ADDISON WES EPTH SERIES

5.99

PARNELL AND THE IRISH QUESTION

Tim Hodge
Series editor: Christopher Culpin

D1392520

LONGMAN

CONTENTS

Part 1   Telling the story   3

Part 2

1 The Irish Question   28

2 Gladstone and Ireland   46

3 What kind of a nationalist was Parnell?   64

4 'Parnellism and crime'   82

5 The fall of Parnell   92

6 An assessment of Parnell's career   104

Further reading   112

Index   115

PART ONE

TELLING THE STORY

He came out, a tall, gaunt figure, thin and deadly pale. He looked straight at me smiling, and his curiously burning eyes looked into mine with a wonderful intentness that threw into my brain the sudden thought: 'This man is wonderful – and different'.

I asked him why he had not answered my last invitation to dinner, and if nothing would induce him to come. He answered that he had not opened his letters for days but if I would let him, he would come to dinner directly he returned from Paris, where he had to go for his sister's wedding.

In leaning forward in the cab to say goodbye a rose I was wearing in my bodice fell out onto my skirt. He picked it up and, touching it lightly with his lips, placed it in his button-hole.

This rose I found long years afterwards done up in an envelope, with my name and the date, among his most private papers, and when he died I laid it upon his heart.

Quoted in Katharine O'Shea, ***Charles Stewart Parnell: His Love Story and Political Life*** *(Cassell, 1914)*

This is how Katharine O'Shea describes her first meeting with Charles Stewart Parnell. Their romance, conducted while she was still married to Captain William O'Shea, was to inspire both a Hollywood film and a television drama series. The revelation of their affair and the ensuing divorce scandal destroyed both his political career and his health. He died in the arms of Katharine soon after their marriage in 1891. He was just 46 years old.

The purpose of this book is to investigate Parnell and his times and to assess his role in the development of Anglo-Irish relations in the nineteenth century.

Figure 1 Charles Stewart Parnell

Figure 2 Katharine O'Shea

You should think about the following questions as you read through the survey of his life and the political and economic events affecting Anglo-Irish relations in the nineteenth century:

▲ What were his aims and motives?

▲ What was the nature of his Irish Nationalism?

▲ How did he lead the Irish in Ireland and in Britain?

▲ How effective was his leadership and was he ultimately a failure?

▲ What is the relationship between Parnell and political and economic developments in Ireland?

A comparison of populations – in millions

Date	Ireland	Mainland Britain
1801	5.2	10.6
1811	5.9	12.1
1821	6.8	14.2
1831	7.7	16.3
1841	8.2	18.5
1851	6.5	20.8
1861	5.8	23.1
1871	5.4	26.1
1881	5.1	29.8
1891	4.7	33.1
1901	4.4	37.0

Figure 3 Ireland in the nineteenth century

Chronology of important events

The life of Charles Stewart Parnell

1846 Born at Avondale, County Wicklow, son of John Henry Parnell and Delia Stewart Parnell

1853 Sent to school in England, first to Yeovil in Somerset, and later, to Kirk Langley in Derbyshire

1859 Inherits Avondale after the death of his father

1865 Becomes an undergraduate at Magdalene College, Cambridge

1869 Suspended from Cambridge after a fight with a manure merchant; never returns

1873 Appointed High Sheriff of County Wicklow

1874 Becomes a member of Isaac Butt's Home Rule League

1875 Enters the House of Commons as MP for Meath

1876 Begins association with tactic of 'obstruction' in the House of Commons

1877 Elected President of Home Rule Confederation

1879 Irish National Land League is founded with Parnell as President

1880 Elected leader of Irish Parliamentary Party (March)
First meeting with Mrs Katharine O'Shea (July)
First suggests policy of 'boycotting' during land war

1881 Advises testing the Land Act (Sept.)
Arrested and imprisoned in Kilmainhaim Jail (Oct.)

1882 Released after negotiations with Gladstone. Agrees to cooperate over the Land Act and control the Land League (May)
Irish National League founded with Parnell as President (Oct.)

1885 Sends Gladstone a draft of his Home Rule Constitution (Oct.)
Advises Irish in Britain to vote Conservative. 86 Irish Nationalists returned exactly equalling Liberal majority. Keeps Conservatives in power

1886 Gladstone becomes PM as Parnell switches support to Liberals after the conversion of Gladstone to the idea of Home Rule (Feb.)
Conservatives returned to power after defeat of Home Rule bill (July)

1886 Disassociates from Plan of Campaign to maintain alliance between Irish Party and the Liberals (Dec.)

1887 *The Times* runs its 'Parnellism and Crime' campaign linking Parnell with terrorism

1888 Parliamentary Commission set up to investigate allegations against Parnell and activities of the Land League

1889 A journalist, Pigott, admits forging Parnell letters. Parnell exonerated (Feb.) Captain O'Shea sues for divorce naming Parnell as co-respondent (Dec.)

1890 Divorce granted. Gladstone and the Liberals oppose Parnell as leader of the Irish Party (Nov.)
Catholic Church in Ireland denounces Parnell. Meetings of Irish MPs end in split; majority opposes Parnell as leader (Dec.)

1891 Fails to gather popular support in Ireland to re-establish his leadership
Marriage of Parnell and Katharine O'Shea (June)
Death of Parnell in Brighton (Oct.)

Political and Economic Events

1800 Act of Union abolishes Irish parliament. Irish MPs to sit at Westminster

1823 Formation of Daniel O'Connell's Catholic Association

1829 Catholic Emancipation Act

1838 Poor Law is introduced in Ireland

1840 O'Connell founds Repeal Association

1843 Meeting at Clontarf banned; O'Connell's credibility destroyed

1845 Beginning of Irish Famine

1848 Failure of Young Ireland rebellion

1850 Irish Tenant League founded

1858 Irish Republican Brotherhood founded by James Stephens in Dublin

1859 Fenian Brotherhood set up in USA

1867 Unsuccessful Fenian revolt in Ireland and Britain

1868 Gladstone announces mission to pacify Ireland after Liberal election

1869 Protestant Irish Church disestablished

1870 Irish Land Act to give protection to tenants

1872 Secret Ballot is introduced

1873 Home Rule League founded by Isaac Butt

1874 Conservatives win election and Disraeli becomes PM

1877 Beginning of agricultural depression; failure of potato crop

1879 Beginning of Land War

1880 Gladstone returns as PM after Liberal election victory

1881 Second Land Act provides tenants' demands; fixity of tenure, fair rent and free sale of tenant's interest (3Fs) (Aug.)
Land League outlawed (Oct.)

1882 Land agitation collapses after 'Kilmainham Treaty' (May)
Phoenix Parks murders of Chief Secretary for Ireland and his Under-Secretary (May)
Arrears Act extends operation of Land Act to those in arrears of rent (Aug.)

1886 Split in Liberal Party causes defeat of Home Rule and Conservatives return to office after election defeat for Gladstone and the Liberals

1888 Land Purchase Act begins process of transferring ownership to tenants

1892 Gladstone forms fourth ministry after election victory for the Liberals

1893 Foundation of Gaelic League which aims to promote 'Irishness' and reject English cultural influences (July)
Rejection of Second Home Rule bill by House of Lords (Sept.)

1896 Foundation of Irish Socialist Republican Party by James Connolly

1898 Irish Local Government Act sets up elected county and district councils

1900 Reunion of Irish Parliamentary Party under John Redmond (Jan.)
Foundation by Arthur Griffith of organisation which becomes Sinn Fein

Parnell's life and political career

Avondale (1846–65)

Charles Stewart Parnell was the seventh child of an American mother and a Protestant Anglo-Irish landlord, John Henry Parnell. He was born at Avondale, the family estate of about 4,000 acres, on 27 June 1846. Although thousands were dying in Ireland at this time of the Great Famine, Avondale, in the prosperous county of Wicklow, was hardly affected by it.

His background suggests an important question:

Why did a member of the privileged Protestant landlord class choose to lead a predominantly Catholic tenant movement?

Biographers of Parnell have grappled with this problem but a satisfactory answer has been difficult to find. Some have looked to the influence of his mother to explain his motives. Delia Stewart was the daughter of a famous American naval hero, who was honoured for the part he played in the 1812 war against Britain. It has been suggested that Charles inherited an anti-British prejudice from his mother. There is little evidence that she had such an attitude towards the British. In fact, her social life centred on Dublin Castle, the seat of British administration. She ensured that her daughters were presented at the court of Queen Victoria!

It seems more likely that Parnell was affected by the tradition of his great-grandfather, Sir John Parnell, and his grandfather, William Parnell. The former had opposed the Union of 1800 and William was known for his sympathy for the rights of Catholics and a genuine concern for his tenants. If Charles was subject to such influence, it was not apparent in those early years at Avondale. He himself admitted that even in early manhood he was not that interested in politics.

However, members of the family testify to aspects of his character in his formative years which are consistent with his style of leadership in later life. His iron will and single-minded determination are revealed in one particular story. He and his sister Fanny used to play a game of soldiers in the nursery; the idea was to roll a ball at the opponent's forces and knock down as many as possible. On one occasion, when it

Figure 4 Avondale, County Wicklow, Ireland

came to Fanny's turn, Charles had taken the precaution of gluing his soldiers to the floor!

Coming of age (1865–75)

There appears to be an aimlessness about Parnell as a young man. He entered Magdalene College, Cambridge at 19, claimed his inheritance of Avondale on reaching 21 and travelled between England, Ireland, France and America before the age of 26. There is little evidence of the development of any political ambition or philosophy during this time.

This was at the time when the ***Fenians*** were active and yet they appear to have had little or no effect on Parnell at the time. Neither was his interest stirred by Gladstone's Irish policy (see Picture Gallery, page 24 and Chapter 2). In Ireland, he busied himself in running the estate and attending the social functions expected of a member of his class. He enjoyed cricket and seems to have played a great deal. He was appointed High Sheriff of County Wicklow in 1873.

Yet his years in England did leave their mark. He was a proud, arrogant man. He recognised his position in Irish society as a member of a privileged elite, with a respected family tradition. He spoke with an English rather than an Irish accent, and stood apart from most Irishmen. But in England he was made to feel different, even inferior. Among the sons of the English gentry at Cambridge University, his identity was clearly Irish. He felt despised and rejected.

It is likely that his experiences at Cambridge fostered an anti-English attitude. Cambridge symbolised for him everything that was disagreeable about English society.

He never completed his degree at Cambridge. After three and a half unproductive years, he was suspended and never returned. The occasion for his suspension was his conviction for assault on a local manure merchant. Although there was a gentle side to his nature, the aggressive tendency was never far from the surface.

Parnell was clearly more comfortable in the role of Irish landlord, but he was no more settled in Ireland. On a visit to Paris in 1871, he met and fell in love with an American beauty, Miss Woods. He fully expected marriage and was devastated on his return to Ireland to receive a letter from Miss Woods announcing her departure to Newport, Rhode Island. This prompted him to set out at once for America in pursuit. Miss Woods rejected him and he was left sullen and dejected. He retreated to Alabama where his brother John had gone out to plant cotton and grow fruit.

There followed two incidents which almost ended his life. He and John were involved in a train crash near Birmingham, Alabama, in which John was injured. Later, in Virginia, Charles was lucky to avoid decapitation in a cage going down a mineshaft. These experiences affected him greatly. He remained extremely superstitious for the rest of his life.

The brothers returned to Ireland in 1872. For the next few years, Charles seemed to have no more ambition than to settle down to life as a country gentleman. There was little to suggest he was destined for the political path which lay ahead.

KEY TERM

The **Fenians** were a revolutionary movement which emerged in the 1860s. They took their name from *Fianna*, a Gaelic word for a legendary band of warrior heroes. The Fenians were founded in Ireland as the Irish Republican Brotherhood in 1858 by James Stephens (see Picture Gallery, page 24). The Fenian Brotherhood was a support organisation based in America among Irish immigrants – the name 'Fenian' applied to both organisations. Its driving force was that England was the cause of all Ireland's problems. Its aim was to bring about an independent Irish Republic, by force if necessary.

A rising was attempted in 1867, but it ended in fiasco. Two incidents in England made the Fenians notorious. In Manchester, in September 1867, a policeman was killed during a successful rescue of two Fenians from a prison van. Part of a wall at Clerkenwell Prison in London was blown up in an attempt to release Fenian prisoners – a number of lives were lost. Arrests followed and three Fenians were executed for the murder of the policeman. Among supporters, they became known as the 'Manchester Martyrs'.

Political apprenticeship (1875–79)

◢ Source A

'My dear boy, we have got a splendid recruit, an historic name, my friend, young Parnell of Wicklow; and unless I am mistaken, the Saxon will find him an ugly customer, though he is a good looking fellow.'

Isaac Butt on Parnell, 1874

◢ Source B

'An Englishman of the strongest type moulded for an Irish purpose.'

Michael Davitt on Parnell, 1877

Both Sources A and B provide evidence of the qualities Parnell was to display later as an Irish nationalist leader. Isaac Butt (see Picture Gallery, page 24) was referring to the occasion when Parnell joined the Home Rule League. Unlike the Fenians, Butt believed that Irish MPs could persuade the British government to grant an Irish parliament within the Union. Michael Davitt (see page 25) was a more radical figure; his aim was to transfer ownership of Irish land to the tenants.

Whatever he became, there is no doubt that Parnell drifted into politics. His first involvement was to support his brother's unsuccessful bid to become MP for Wicklow in 1874. He joined the Home Rule League and supported the idea of protecting the rights of tenants. He then decided to put himself forward as a candidate for the House of Commons. His first attempts at public speaking were stumbling and awkward. He was defeated in the election for County Dublin in 1874.

It seems that this defeat finally fired his ambition. He was determined to stand again and win. He used the family name to take a leading role in the Home Rule League, and forced himself to speak more effectively. He made up for lost time by doing his political homework. He now had a sense of purpose.

His opportunity came suddenly with the death of the MP for Meath in 1875. He was adopted as a Home Rule candidate and his campaign was more effective this time. He won convincingly and entered the House of Commons in April 1875.

Parnell did not distinguish himself in his early days as an MP. His speeches were still hesitant and ineffective. He soon became frustrated by Butt's leadership of the Home Rule Party. He wanted a more forceful approach. Taking his cue from Joseph Biggar, he began to adopt an **'obstructionist' policy** and became the master of the technique. He once said of the British government: 'They will do what we can make them do.' Already he was more concerned about the effect of his actions in parliament on the masses in Ireland. Butt was increasingly sidelined.

Parnell was first elected President of the Home Rule Confederation of Great Britain in 1877. He had secret contacts with a number of leading Fenians without ever committing himself to their policy. His aloofness was one of his great strengths. He was poised to bid for the leadership of the parliamentary party when events in Ireland presented him with another opportunity.

KEY TERM

'Obstructionist' policy: under the leadership of Isaac Butt, Irish MPs formed a loose organisation. Butt's approach was to cooperate with the British authorities, based on a respect for parliamentary traditions. At heart, he was a conservative. However, there was a handful of Fenians within the Party who believed Butt's approach would achieve nothing. They began to use the rules of parliamentary procedure to their advantage. Joseph Biggar, for instance, spoke for four hours on 22 April 1875 reading extracts from newspapers and government records. He deliberately 'obstructed' the business of parliament to stop measures going through and force attention on Irish issues. While Butt disapproved and was embarrassed by this, Parnell watched with interest. In 1877 the government moved to pass the South Africa Bill to legalise the annexation of the Transvaal. Seven Irishmen, including Parnell, forced the House of Commons to sit continuously for 45 hours by relays of speeches.

The New Departure (1879–82)

The period from 1879 to 1882 was the most dramatic of Parnell's political career. He already appreciated the weakness of a minority party in parliament without mass support in Ireland and he realised the potential of financial backing from Irish America. The phrase 'a new departure' was coined to describe a formidable alliance. This would consist of three strands:

- an independent, disciplined Irish party speaking as one voice on Irish matters in the House of Commons;
- a popular mass nationalist movement at home;
- enlisting the support of the influential Clan-na-Gael, the Irish American organisation.

This presented enormous difficulties because there were different ambitions and aims within and between the different strands. Parnell remained aloof and vague about whether Home Rule or total separation from Britain was the ultimate goal. There was, however, an understanding of short-term aims:

1 An agreement to work for a Home Rule Parliament
2 Protection of tenants from the threat of eviction
3 Transfer of ownership from landlords to tenants.

It is unlikely that Parnell was clear in his own mind about priorities. The key for him was to be effective, to achieve something for Ireland. He had quickly developed the skills of the practical politician and he chose his words carefully depending on the audience. If others could get things moving, his determination and will to win could achieve results.

This was the situation when a crisis on the land loomed in 1879. Agricultural depression brought a slump in prices. Unable to pay their rents, tenant farmers were threatened with eviction. With the failure of the potato crop, the threat of mass starvation was once again felt in Ireland. Michael Davitt was the first to see the opportunity. If the tenant farmers were organised to resist eviction and force landlords to accept reduced rents, a powerful national organisation could be mobilised. Davitt wasted no time in turning the spontaneous resistance of peasants in County Mayo into a national body and enlisting Parnell's support. In October 1879, the National Land League of Ireland was formed with Parnell as President.

During the 'land war' which followed, the Land League represented a revolutionary alternative to official authority. Evictions were resisted by force, shelter and support were provided for those who were evicted and Land League courts decided on a fair level of rent. Officially, violence was deplored, but members were clearly involved in intimidation and even murder of landlords. Tenants who agreed to pay 'excessive' rents or accepted the tenancy of a holding which had become available as a result of eviction were punished. Shots were fired into thighs and pieces of ear removed. Parnell took care to distance himself and the organisation from such activity. He suggested, instead, that enemies of the Land League should be sent to 'moral' Coventry: they should be denied all social and commercial contact with their neighbours. The first notable victim was a Captain Boycott who was forced to bring in 50 **Orangemen** from Ulster to bring in the harvest. His name gave rise to a new word in the English language.

The New Departure was working. The British parliament was forced to respond to the situation in Ireland and take the Irish parliamentary party seriously. Butt died in 1879 and was replaced as leader by the moderate William Shaw. However, the general election of 1880 increased the support for Parnell and he was elected leader of the Party in May 1880. He was now both leader of a mass movement and the Party in parliament. His first decision was to sit in opposition to

Gladstone's new Liberal government, to emphasise the independence of the Party.

KEY TERM

Orangemen were followers of the Orange Order, a secret society rather like the Freemasons. The Orange Order was founded in 1795. It took its name from William of Orange (William III), who was a great hero to the Protestants of Ulster. It was William who had relieved Londonderry from the siege laid to it by the forces of the Catholic James II. At the battle of the Boyne in 1690, he defeated James and the Protestant succession to the throne was secured. The Orange Order was a fiercely anti-Catholic organisation. It saw its role as protecting Protestant interests against any real or imaginary threats from Catholics. During the nineteenth century, it gained some respectability and became increasingly identified with loyalty to the Union with Great Britain. This meant opposition to any form of Irish Nationalism; during the Home Rule crisis of 1886, the Orange Order was behind mass demonstrations to oppose it. This opposition was repeated in 1892 and again in 1912. Their attitude can be summed up in a favourite slogan: 'No Surrender'.

The new Liberal government was forced to deal with the crisis in Ireland. Their first priority was to restore law and order. While Gladstone was considering a constructive policy of land reform, he first introduced a Coercion Bill giving special powers to the police and military authorities. Parnell used the opportunity to strengthen his hold over the Irish Party and mould it into a more disciplined body. The Coercion Bill was obstructed until 36 Irish members, including Parnell, were suspended. The introduction of the Land Act presented him with difficulties. He recognised the benefits of it for the tenant farmers while it did not go far enough for the extremists in the Land League. In the short term Parnell had to show more opposition to it than he felt (see Chapter 3).

Parnell's refusal to cooperate over the Land Act brought matters to a head. The government played into his hands. He was arrested and imprisoned in Kilmainham Jail in Dublin. This suited his purpose well. He could be seen as a martyr to the cause of Irish Nationalism. At the same time he realised that the tenant farmers were keen to take advantage of the Land Act and the crisis on the land was coming to an end with the return of better potato harvests. He could show himself as the only one who could control the violence and focus the forces under his control on the goal of a Home Rule parliament.

Parnell could achieve none of this while in prison. It was not in Gladstone's interest either. He wanted to give his Land Act a chance to work. Negotiations were conducted informally through intermediaries and a compromise was reached. Under the 'Kilmainham Treaty', as it became known, Parnell agreed to use his influence to control the activities of the Land League and encourage cooperation with the new land legislation. For his part, Gladstone agreed to release Parnell and include in the provisions of the Act tenants in arrears of rent. There was a personal reason why Parnell wished to return to England. He had begun an affair with Katharine O'Shea, the wife of Captain O'Shea, a member of Parnell's party. She was expecting their first baby.

The agreement between Parnell and Gladstone was almost wrecked within days of his release. In Phoenix Park in Dublin the Chief Secretary, Lord Frederick Cavendish, and Thomas Burke, his Under-Secretary were stabbed to death with long surgical knives in May 1882. It looked as if any hope of cooperation with the Liberals over Home Rule was, at least, delayed.

Home Rule (1882–86)

Parnell wasted no time in carrying out his part of the deal. He wound up the Land League and quickly replaced it with the Irish National League. To some this represented a betrayal: his biggest critic was his own sister Anna (see Picture Gallery, page 25 and Chapter 3), who had organised the Ladies Land League during his imprisonment. Parnell's view was that the situation had changed and required a different approach.

He wanted to channel the anti-government feeling stirred up during the land war into the national issue. To the moderates in his party and to the British government he appeared to make Home Rule the limit of his aims. To the more extreme elements he could present Home Rule as a means to the end of total separation. As always, he presented an air of mystery and remained vague about his real intentions. These are no more clear to us today. He kept no private papers and his letters to Katharine O'Shea and others provide no real clue. His public speeches on the matter depended on who he was talking to (see Chapter 3). His great skill was to keep such different forces together and present a united front. The new National League gave him the national structure to endorse candidates for elections and campaign effectively at constituency level. His authority over the party was increased and he could forge a tighter, more disciplined body. The Irish Parliamentary Party was in good shape to fight the General Election of 1885.

Parnell could see the advantage of controlling a disciplined group of Irish MPs. Before the election of 1885, he commanded a party of 60. He realised that the best hope for Home Rule was to hold the balance between the two main parties in the House of Commons. This meant he had to be seen as independent of both of them. In the case of a close election result he could offer support to either one in return for Home Rule. As the election approached, he calculated that there was more chance of progress with the Conservatives than the Liberals. A young Conservative, Lord Randolph Churchill (see Picture Gallery, page 25), seemed to be offering the promise of concessions to Irish demands in return for Irish votes. In June 1885 the Liberals were defeated by a combination of Irish and Conservatives, and Gladstone resigned. A Conservative government was formed with Lord Salisbury as Prime Minister.

Almost immediately the coercion measures were dropped and an act was passed to allow tenants to buy land on easy terms. Parnell was delighted and instructed Irishmen in Britain to vote Conservative. The reform measures of 1884–85 significantly increased the size of the Irish electorate and Parnell was confident of increasing the size of his parliamentary party. The election result was perhaps the strangest in British history: the Liberal majority of 86 over the Conservatives was exactly matched by the return of 86 Irish Nationalists.

Parnell was able to keep Salisbury in power, but it soon became clear that the Conservatives would not go so far as to agree to Home Rule. Everything now depended on Gladstone (see Chapter 2). Privately he had decided that Home Rule was necessary, but he was concerned that there was too much opposition to it within his own party; he was hoping that the Conservatives would introduce it. When it was clear that this was not going to happen in December 1885, Herbert Gladstone decided to announce to the press that his father was converted to the idea of Home Rule. Parnell immediately switched support to the Liberals and defeated the Conservatives. Gladstone became

Prime Minister for the third time in January 1886, but the prospects were not good. Both wings of the Liberal Party were opposed to Home Rule. When it was introduced in the House of Commons in April, it met fierce opposition from many sides. Lord Randolph Churchill stirred up the religious prejudice of the Orange Order and both Lord Hartington and Joseph Chamberlain (see Picture Gallery, page 26 and Chapter 2), representing different factions within the Liberal Party, were united against it. The bill was defeated by 30 votes; 93 Liberals voted against it.

This sequence of events served neither Gladstone nor Parnell well. Gladstone appealed to the country by calling a general election. Public opinion in Britain was clear. The Liberals were heavily defeated and seriously split. The Liberal Unionists sat in parliament as a separate group. Many later joined the Conservatives, including Joseph Chamberlain. A period of Conservative rule followed. They were now as committed to the Union as the Liberals were to Home Rule. Parnell and his party had now effectively lost their independence. They were firmly wedded to the Liberal Party and that party was to have few prospects of power for the next 20 years.

Parnellism and crime (1887–90)

With the return of the Conservatives to power in 1886, Parnell knew that he must wait until the Irish Party once again held the balance between the two main parties or the Liberals were returned to office. In fact, he was not to live long enough to see that day. The new government was determined to deal firmly with any unrest in Ireland. In response to the 'Plan of Campaign' organised by William O'Brien and John Dillon, a new Crimes Act was passed in 1887. Salisbury's nephew, Arthur Balfour, was appointed Chief Secretary and soon earned the nickname 'Bloody Balfour' for his ruthless determination to use to the full the powers of the new legislation.

The Times took it upon itself to discredit Parnell. It had always been outspoken on Irish matters and took a clear anti-Nationalist position. Parnell himself was at this time withdrawn from the political scene, spending more and more time with Katharine. He refused to associate with the Plan of Campaign believing that there was little to be gained from such direct action; the tactics of the Land League were buried in

1882. It was ironic then that those days should be dragged up again. In April 1887, *The Times* published a letter supposed to have been written by Parnell in 1882 expressing approval of the Phoenix Park murders (see Chapter 4). Parnell immediately dismissed it as a forgery and took out a libel case against the newspaper. More alleged letters were produced; for months the paper was full of letters and articles determined to prove Parnell's implication in violence and crime during his Land League days.

The Conservative government agreed to set up a commission to investigate the whole question. While there was undoubted evidence that the Land League was involved in violence and intimidation, Parnell himself was cleared. Under cross-examination, Richard Pigott, a journalist, admitted forgery. He later fully confessed his guilt and shot himself in a Madrid hotel room. This almost ruined the newspaper. The inquiry cost *The Times* £200,000 (about £10 million today) and it seriously damaged its reputation for fair and factual reporting. Meanwhile, Parnell enjoyed increased authority and prestige. He received a standing ovation from the House of Commons and a great deal of sympathy from the British public. He liked to refer to himself as 'the King' in his letters to his 'very own Queenie', Katharine. At this moment in 1890, he appeared as the 'Uncrowned King of Ireland'.

The divorce scandal (1890–91)

Just when Parnell seemed to be at the height of his power, disaster struck. His affair with Katharine O'Shea had been going on for 10 years. It seems highly probable that Captain O'Shea had known about it for sometime. However, his constant need for money is the likely explanation why he chose not to sue for divorce sooner. Katharine's aunt, Mrs Benjamin Wood, was very rich and Katharine expected to inherit her fortune. Captain O'Shea hoped to receive his share. It was therefore in his interest to keep quiet until the old lady died. When she did die in 1889, it was not long before he sued his wife for divorce on the grounds of adultery with Parnell.

The public scandal of the divorce destroyed Parnell's career and probably contributed to his early death (see Chapter 5). While affairs conducted discreetly were acceptable, the Victorian moral code took a very different view of public revelations in the divorce courts. Both Parnell and Katharine chose not to appear in court, although they entered a counter-charge of adultery against O'Shea with Katharine's sister. Nevertheless, the details of how the affair was conducted were reported in the press and music-hall entertainers wasted no opportunity for cruel jokes at Parnell's expense. It seems that Parnell believed he could keep his private and political life separate. He had not bargained for the devastating consequences of this public scandal. Powerful forces were at work in both Ireland and England.

At first, the Irish parliamentary party unanimously confirmed him as leader. Then Gladstone announced that if he were to remain so, his own leadership of the Liberal Party was in doubt. Nonconformist opinion was at the heart of the Liberal Party. Many Irish MPs knew that the party could achieve little without the support of the Liberals despite the appearance of independence. Meanwhile, the Irish Catholic Church denounced Parnell as an adulterer. As a Protestant, he had been careful to ensure that his movement had the support of the Catholic Church. With that removed he could no longer rely on the support of the majority of the Irish people. The crisis came to a head at a stormy meeting of the Irish members in Committee Room 15 of the House of Commons in December 1890. Eventually, a majority of 45 to 29 decided to depose Parnell as leader. The split between Parnellites and anti-Parnellites was not to be healed for another ten years, leaving the party weak and ineffective.

True to his nature, Parnell refused to accept the decision and go quietly. He still believed that the force of his personality was greater than the forces lined up against him. In a desperate bid to re-establish his leadership he campaigned in Ireland. He fought three by-elections in succession, but each time he was defeated; on one occasion he had lime thrown in his eyes. His refusal to accept defeat became almost obsessive. In his desperation he appealed to the more radical Nationalists, the Fenians and Landleaguers. His speeches became more violent.

Parnell's health had always been weak and the physical demands of the campaign were exhausting. His health was deteriorating. He had married Katharine soon after the divorce and had been shuttling to and fro between their home in Hove, Sussex, and Ireland. Finally, he left Ireland at the end of September 1891 and spent the next week at home with Katharine.

He died in the arms of his wife on 6 October and his body was transported back to Ireland for burial at Glasnevin cemetery in Dublin. He was given the funeral of a nationalist hero. It remained to be seen whether the idea of Home Rule as a permanent settlement of the Irish Question would survive without him.

William Ewart GLADSTONE, *1809–98*

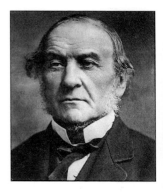

Gladstone served as Liberal Prime Minister 1868–74, 1880–85, 1886 and 1892–94. He attempted a constructive policy in Ireland to remove Catholic grievances. He disestablished the Church of Ireland in 1869 and passed the Land Acts of 1870 and 1881. He split his party and lost the 1886 election over his conversion to Home Rule. His second Home Rule bill passed the Commons but was defeated in the House of Lords in 1893. He retired to his estate at Hawarden in Wales in 1894.

James STEPHENS, *1825–1901*

As a member of Young Ireland in 1848 Stephens became convinced of the possibility of an Irish Nationalist revolution. He founded the Irish Republican Brotherhood in 1858 and visited the USA to raise awareness and financial support. He founded *The Irish People* newspaper in 1863 and planned the abortive Fenian Rising of 1865. Lived in Paris and returned to Ireland in 1885 when he retired from public life until his death.

Isaac BUTT, *1813–79*

Butt was founder of the Home Government Association in 1870. Lawyer and Professor of political economy, he came from a Tory and Protestant Unionist background. He defended both Young Irelanders in 1848 and Fenians in the 1860s. Impressed by their sincerity as Nationalists, if not their commitment to violence, he became convinced of the need for Home Rule for Ireland. However, he was ineffective as leader of the Irish group in parliament. It remained a loose organisation under his leadership. On one wing were the ex-Fenians, while others were really Irish Liberals and even Tories. His traditional respect for the law was a source of frustration to some of the more radical members of his party. His death marked the end of the polite approach to Home Rule and gave Parnell his chance to lead a more forceful and effective parliamentary party.

Michael DAVITT, *1846–1906*

Born in County Mayo, Davitt emigrated to Lancashire and lost his right arm in a mill accident at 11. Joined the Fenians in 1865 and was imprisoned in Dartmoor for his involvement in the Rising. Released in 1877, he saw the potential of combining the agitation for land reform and the nationalist movement. He was the prime mover behind the founding of the Land League in 1879 and persuading Parnell to front the organisation. He was also influential in maintaining links with Nationalists in the United States. He opposed Parnell during the crisis of 1890–91 and served as an anti-Parnellite MP in the 1890s. His working-class background and socialist leanings became more evident. He visited the leaders of the Russian revolutionary party in 1903 and published *The Fall of Feudalism in Ireland* in 1904.

Anna PARNELL, *1852–1911*

Anna was the sister of Charles Stewart. She organised a famine relief fund in 1879 and established, with her sister Fanny, the Ladies Land League. Anna worked unstintingly on behalf of peasants threatened with eviction especially when her brother was in prison. Felt betrayed by him when he suppressed the organisation on his release. Refused to speak to him again. She expressed her feelings about the Land League in a manuscript, 'The Great Sham', which was not published until the 1950s, many years after her death. She retired from public life in the 1880s and spent much of her life in England. She was drowned off Ilfracombe in 1911 and buried in a lonely grave in the local churchyard.

Lord Randolph Henry Spencer CHURCHILL, *1849–95*

Third son of the Duke of Marlborough of Blenheim, MP for Woodstock in 1874. Randolph became associated with the philosophy of Tory Democracy and was a fierce opponent of Gladstone. He was instrumental in forging an alliance with Parnell's party in 1885 to win power for the Conservatives. When Gladstone announced his conversion to Home Rule, Churchill played the 'Orange card' by stirring Ulster's protestants into opposition to the measure.

A rising star of the party, Churchill became Chancellor of the Exchequer at the age of 37. Resigned after a few months in office over a disagreement with PM Lord Salisbury and his Cabinet, never to return to office. He died of syphilis in 1895. Father of Winston Churchill.

Joseph CHAMBERLAIN *1836–1914*

Radical mayor of Birmingham and Liberal MP. Acted as an intermediary over the Kilmainhaim Treaty in 1882; opposed Home Rule because of his belief in the integrity of the Empire, though he continued to believe in measures of local government short of Home Rule. Joined the Liberal Unionists after the split in 1886 and took office under Lord Salisbury in 1895 as Colonial Secretary. Resigned in 1903 to campaign for tariff reform as part of his commitment to the idea of imperial preference. Often blamed for splitting the Conservative Party over the issue and causing the Liberal landslide victory of 1906.

Patterned notes

One of the most difficult skills to master is how to make good notes. You need to be clear about the reasons for taking notes before deciding what to record and how to record it. We cannot keep in our head everything we read. The more we read the more difficult it is to recall every detail. Yet you have to face examinations which expect you to remember enough information to support logical arguments. It's very tempting to write too many notes; a fat file can give you a sense of security! But it doesn't solve the problem – how to get enough information in your head.

Taking notes should be seen as an essential part of preparing for the examination. In that sense, revision starts almost as soon as you begin the course. It involves reviewing what you've read and the work you've done. By the end of the course you need to have a manageable amount of information to learn. The key is to have a clear focus for the notes you take. This is best achieved by answering a question and 'brainstorming' the answer. Patterned notes allow the opportunity to limit the notes you take and focus on the key issues and the links between them.

Complete the diagram below, which has been started for you. Keep to the focus provided by the question in the middle of the diagram. To begin with, rely only on your memory of what you've read in Part One. Then look for anything in the chapter which you've missed. Remember that you are only looking for ideas and information which strictly answer the question.

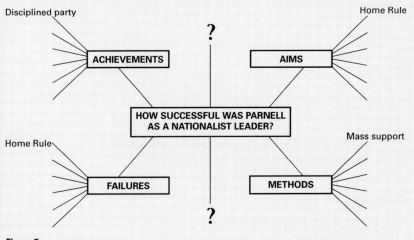

Figure 5

CHAPTER ONE

THE IRISH QUESTION

Objectives

⬕ To understand the nature of the Irish Question as it developed between 1800 and 1868

⬕ To consider the effectiveness of British rule in Ireland from the Union to 1868

⬕ To study the effect of Catholic Emancipation and the attempts to Repeal the Act of Union

⬕ To consider the consequences of the Famine, 1845–68.

Before we can assess the role of Parnell, we must know what is meant by the term 'The Irish Question'. As is often the case, it is much easier to ask the question than to find the answer. The question is straightforward enough:

What should be the relationship between Britain and Ireland?

This chapter will examine the relationship between Britain and Ireland at about the time Ireland became part of Britain under the terms of the Act of Union of 1800. It will go on to trace the development of that relationship between 1800 and 1868. The first of these tasks requires consideration of a number of different strands of the relationship:

⬕ religion
⬕ economy and society
⬕ politics

These will be dealt with separately. As you read through the sections, think about the following points:

⬕ the many ways in which these strands are linked;
⬕ the grievances felt by many Irish people;
⬕ the difficulty of finding an answer to the Irish Question.

Religion

There were three main religious groups in Ireland: Catholics, Anglicans (Church of Ireland) and Presbyterians. There are no precise figures available for 1800, but a reasonable estimate can be made. In a population of about 5 million, around 80 per cent were Catholic. The rest were Protestant, with slightly greater numbers of Anglicans compared with Presbyterians. This is important because religion for the Irish was at the centre of their personal lives and was one of the barriers separating them from each other.

The native Irish were exclusively Catholic, while settlers from England and Scotland belonged to the two Protestant denominations. The religious wars of the seventeenth century had confirmed the Anglican Church as the established Church of Ireland. As a symbol of England's power over the defeated Catholics, it held a privileged position in Ireland. It was the church of the conquerors, supported by the British government.

Penal laws, introduced in the eighteenth century, discriminated against Catholics. For instance, Catholics were denied the right to own land by an act of 1704 and the right to vote was taken away in 1728. Although these penal laws had been relaxed by 1800, Catholic grievances remained.

The Act of Union of 1800 reaffirmed the privileged position of the Anglican Church. The Church tax, the **tithe**, was collected from all Irish people to support the Church of Ireland which was attended by just 10 per cent of the population. Although some Catholics could now vote, they could not hold public office. All of Ireland's MPs (100 in 1801) were Protestant.

Key Term

Tithe literally means 'tenth'. By law, everyone was required to pay one-tenth of their annual wealth to the Church of England in tax.

Economy and society

In 1800 Ireland was experiencing a population explosion. The population increased from about 4 million in 1780 to 6.7 million in 1821. There were few towns of any size besides Dublin, Belfast and Cork. The vast majority of people lived in rural communities and made a living from the land. There were a few Catholic landowners, but the penal laws meant that most landlords were members of the

Anglican minority. They were a small privileged group. The native population were mainly either farm labourers or tenant farmers. Broadly speaking, the economic and social differences reflected the religious divide. Even in Ulster, where the Presbyterians were concentrated, the aristocracy was dominated by Anglicans.

In the 20 years before 1800, the Irish economy was enjoying something of a boom. Some of the larger tenant farmers were able to share in the increased prosperity of the landlords. However, the lowest classes gained little or no benefit. They made up a high proportion of the total population. They lived in appalling conditions: one-roomed mud cabins, with natural earth floors, no windows and no chimneys.

Ireland's economy and society were therefore insecure. The greatest weakness was lack of capital to invest in either agriculture or industry. It has been estimated that more than 80 per cent of the wealth created in Ireland was going out of the island each year. Most of this was in the form of rents to landlords living in England. This was dangerous. Whereas, in Britain, the increased population could be absorbed in the factories and mines of the Industrial Revolution, Ireland experienced little industrialisation. It remained heavily dependent on agriculture. As greater profits could be gained from rearing animals than growing crops, less land was available for cultivation. As the population increased, there were less opportunities for employment. Too many people relied on a single source of food: the potato.

There was a great deal of social unrest among the Irish peasantry. This took various forms of violence and intimidation. Secret societies, with names like 'Whiteboys' or 'Molly Maguires', set fire to property, maimed animals, sent threatening letters and even carried out 'assassinations'. The victims were not just Protestants. Catholic landlords and better-off tenants were also targets. It was more a case of the 'have-nots' against the 'haves'.

Politics

There had been a separate Irish parliament, based on the English model, since the thirteenth century. In fact, its powers were very limited. The real power was in the hands of the Lord Lieutenant appointed by the British government. Inspired by the example of the American rebels against British rule and their success in the subsequent

War of Independence, Protestant 'Patriots' campaigned for a parliament which would have the power to make laws for Ireland. The leader of the 'Patriots', Henry Grattan, believed that a great victory had been won when the British government conceded *legislative* independence in 1782.

This proved to be an illusion. In theory, the Irish parliament could pass laws without the consent of the government in Great Britain. However, the Crown held the right to veto any legislation. More importantly, the Lord Lieutenant (the Crown's representative in Ireland) was not subject to the control of the Irish parliament. In reality, the reverse was the case. He could control the Irish parliament through influence, the promise of rewards and electoral corruption. 'Grattan's Parliament' achieved little during its short existence: it lasted just 18 years.

Demands for electoral reform and rights for Catholics are evidence of the failure of the Irish parliament to represent the Irish people. It was divided over whether to grant concessions to Catholics. It was the British Prime Minister, William Pitt, who forced through reforms. With the outbreak of war against revolutionary France in 1793, he was afraid of an anti-government alliance of Catholics and Presbyterians. In 1793 Catholics were granted the right to vote and to hold official positions except the right to become MPs.

It was against this background that a young Protestant lawyer, Wolfe Tone, led the Society of United Irishmen into an armed rebellion against British rule in 1798. The involvement of the French made it potentially very dangerous to British security, already at war with France. The age-old fear of Ireland being used as a base for Britain's enemies to attack the mainland seemed to have become a reality. In fact, the rising was poorly planned and easily put down.

The revolt was fought in the name of Irishmen united by nationality rather than divided by religion. In fact, it degenerated into sectarian violence in places. It convinced many within the governing classes that a closer association between Ireland and Britain would serve the interests of both islands. Despite the vocal opposition within the Irish parliament to the idea of Direct Rule, it eventually agreed to its own abolition in 1800. The British government was determined to get its way. It used influence, pressure and bribery to build up support for

Union. Anti-Unionists had no alternative policy. The Act of Union became law in August 1800.

By the terms of the Act, all Ireland's affairs were the responsibility of the British government in London. One hundred MPs were elected in Ireland to the House of Commons in Westminster; 32 Irish peers were to sit in the House of Lords. Catholic emancipation had been promised but not granted. King George III refused to agree to it on the grounds that it would be against his coronation oath to uphold the Church of England. The Union was not a 'happy marriage', entered into willingly by both partners for their mutual benefit. Primarily, it served the interests of Britain. Tighter control over Ireland gave a greater sense of security to the British establishment. Irish Protestants increasingly felt that their privileges could be better protected through preservation of the Union.

Without Catholic emancipation, it was unlikely that the Catholic majority would see themselves as loyal subjects of the British Crown. In fact, when Napoleon escaped from Elba in 1815, there was popular rejoicing in Ireland.

The Irish Question (1800–1868)

The most dramatic episode in the history of Ireland in this period was the **famine** which raged between 1845 and 1847. To many Irish Nationalists it became the symbol of the failure of British rule in Ireland. As Britain had taken responsibility for Ireland in 1800, it was argued, then Britain must be responsible for the deaths from starvation of over one million Irish people. If Ireland had been responsible for its own affairs, the disaster would have been avoided. The reality was far more complex than this. However, it does raise the important question:

How effective was British rule during this period?

Catholic emancipation

Once the Act of Union was passed, British governments faced the problem that British interests as a whole were paramount. Legislation of any sort had first to be agreed by the House of Commons. This was dominated by the English landowning class. Like George III and his son, the Prince Regent, the majority remained opposed to the idea of granting full political rights to Catholics. There was still a great deal of popular prejudice in England. William Pitt realised that to deny Catholics in Ireland full political and civil rights would foster a sense of social injustice and make the Union insecure, but he failed to persuade the political classes that emancipation was necessary. When other enlightened attempts were made to introduce such a measure, they were consistently rejected in the House of Commons in the first two decades after the Union. When in 1821 such a measure did pass the Commons, it was rejected in the House of Lords.

It was in this context that Daniel O'Connell set up the Catholic Association in 1823. He realised that pressure had to be applied on the British establishment by Irish Catholics themselves. His organisation was important because it represented the popular voice of Ireland through peaceful constitutional means. Its aim was to advance the interests of the whole Catholic community. To do this, the support of the Irish Catholic Church was crucial. Popular opinion in Ireland had been dogged by local and sectional interests before O'Connell. Now Ireland had, perhaps for the first time, a genuinely national movement with clear aims and objectives. It asked from its members no more than a penny a month. A mark of its popular support can be gauged from the fact that this 'Catholic Rent' raised £1,000 a week.

O'Connell realised that pressure had to be applied on the British government if changes in the interest of the Catholic majority were to be won. This was to be a recurring theme throughout the existence of the Union. Governments did try to introduce reforms in Ireland, so it would be wrong to accuse them of neglecting Irish matters. Robert Peel, as Chief Secretary, passed the Peace Preservation Act in 1814. This set up a body of professional police and salaried magistrates. There were also tariff and legal reforms. However, these reforms could not solve the fundamental economic and social problems in Ireland. Given the prejudices among both the electorate and in Westminster, governments had little freedom to carry out any far-reaching reforms. Again and again, they resorted to Coercion Acts as a matter of course to deal with social unrest.

O'Connell was determined to bring the question of Catholic emancipation to a head. The opportunity came with the Tory government in almost total disarray after the retirement of Lord Liverpool in 1827. The Cabinet was divided over the issue while the repeal of the Test and Corporations Act in 1828, which removed all civil and legal restrictions on Protestant dissenters, opened them to the charge of religious bias. A by-election in County Clare suddenly provided the battleground. Under the rules of the time, anyone who was appointed to a ministerial position had to seek re-election in his constituency. Early in 1828 Vesey Fitzgerald was appointed President of the Board of Trade and was forced to fight an election. O'Connell decided to stand against him.

As a Catholic there was nothing to prevent him doing this; the problem would come when he tried to take his seat in parliament after his election. This was exactly what he hoped would happen and did happen. The election was a personal triumph; he gained over 2,000 votes to Fitzgerald's 982. This was in spite of an election system which allowed landowners enormous opportunities to influence the electorate. The Duke of Wellington believed that as the Prime Minister he could not risk the prospect of serious social unrest and violence in Ireland if emancipation were not granted. He used this to persuade a reluctant Peel to get the measure through the Commons while he used his own influence to force agreement from both the Lords and King George IV.

The Roman Catholic Emancipation Act of 1829 granted full civil and political rights to Roman Catholics, which meant that they could now become MPs and even occupy ministerial positions. However, O'Connell was denied the right to take his seat immediately on the grounds that the law was not in force when the election was held. He had to fight the seat all over again. Furthermore, the franchise was raised from a 40-shilling freehold to a ten-pound householder suffrage. The Irish electorate was savagely reduced to one-sixth of its former size. The only conclusion that could be drawn in Ireland was that the government was being deliberately spiteful. In fact, it was a desperate measure to reconcile its own supporters; 140 Tories had voted against the Emancipation bill and the Party was in danger of breaking up. This vital reform was granted reluctantly and against the background of traditional fears and prejudice.

O'Connell does not appear to have felt that the restrictions were important. He was triumphant. He made a point of trying to take his seat only to be faced by the oaths of royal supremacy over religious matters and passages referring to the superstitious nature of the Catholic religion which all MPs had to take before the requirement was removed by the Emancipation Act. O'Connell made a point of refusing to take the oath and returned to Clare to face the electorate again. He was elected unopposed and could now legally take his seat. He was not the first Catholic to enter Parliament, as Catholic peers like the Duke of Norfolk had already taken their seats in the House of Lords.

◢ Source

His victory meant much more than that Catholics could now sit in Parliament and become judges. The real victory consisted in the fact that the down-trodden Catholic masses had taken on the government and won. They had won by organisation and discipline, by courage and leadership, by keeping just on the right side of the law and a long way on the right side of loyalty ... And in the first flush of this victory, it either escaped them or seemed unimportant that the victory brought no real change to their everyday lives. In any case, the new strength by which they had won Emancipation could presumably be brought to bear on other issues too.

*Quoted in Robert Kee, **The Green Flag – A History of Irish Nationalism** (Weidenfeld and Nicolson, 1972)*

O'Connell and Repeal
The Whig Reforms (1830–40)

It was the existence of the Union itself which became the target for O'Connell and his organisation. In this campaign, he was to meet stiffer resistance from a British government determined to preserve the Union. However, the Reform crisis in Britain had produced a new situation: it had brought to power a Whig government for the first time in the century. The Whigs had been supporters of Catholic rights during debates on emancipation and O'Connell could expect further concessions from them. He soon realised that there was no prospect of achieving repeal using the techniques which had won emancipation. After the Reform Act of 1832, O'Connell commanded a group of 39 Irish MPs in favour of Repeal, but there was no support for the idea outside this group in the House of Commons. In 1834, a resolution on the issue was defeated by 523 votes to 38. O'Connell would have to bide his time and gain whatever he could from the Whigs.

The Whigs in the 1830s did go some way to address Irish grievances. A grant for education was made in 1831. The Irish Church Act of the same year reformed the unrepresentative Church of Ireland. A number of positions in the Church were abolished by reducing the number of sees and archbishoprics. On the other hand, the Whigs were quite prepared to use coercion to deal with the 'tithe war' during the early years of the decade. Many Catholic farmers refused to pay the tithe to the Anglican Church and the hated tax was forcibly collected by police and the army. The Coercion Act of 1833 aimed to deal with this new outbreak of violence and social unrest.

However, it was soon clear that the Whigs and the Irish needed each other. To prevent the Conservative government of Sir Robert Peel staying in office, the Lichfield House Compact was agreed in 1835. This alliance of Whigs, Radicals and Irish ensured that Peel's minority government lasted only 'a hundred days' and the Whigs were restored to power for the rest of the decade. Under this arrangement, coercion was relaxed and reforms continued. The Irish Under-Secretary, Thomas Drummond, made great efforts to ensure that Catholics were appointed to high office and encouraged them to join the police force. He was prepared to curb the powers of the Orange Order and to consider the rights of tenants as well as landlords. An Act of 1838 changed the tithe to an additional rent charge payable by the landlord.

Further reforms mirrored those in England. A new Poor Law was introduced in 1838 and led to the building of 100 workhouses. Local government was reformed and made more accessible to Catholics under the Corporations Act of 1840. O'Connell himself became Lord Mayor of Dublin in 1841. However, there was an increasing frustration being felt within the support for O'Connell. It appeared that the Whigs were the real winners from the deal. They were kept in office while the Irish were forced to compromise. None of the reforms dealt with the fundamental problems in the Irish economy and society. The tithe may have been hidden but it was still collected indirectly from Catholics and Presbyterians; the economy had not developed and peasants were dangerously vulnerable to starvation. The interests of the Protestant

Ascendancy were still protected by the Union. Unless O'Connell changed tactics and gave hope of real benefits for the Irish people, he was in danger of losing the support of his own people.

O'Connell and Peel (1840–44)

When it became clear that the Whigs were losing their hold on power, O'Connell was happy to return to the theme of Repeal. Faced with a Conservative rather than a Whig government, he had no need to make any deals. In any case, he had to re-establish his leadership of Irish opinion. He founded the Repeal Association in 1840 and modelled it on the old Catholic Association. There was, however, a great deal of uncertainty about the precise constitutional arrangement Repeal implied. It could not mean a return to the position of 1800 since both the Emancipation Act and the Reform Act meant that any Irish parliament would be dominated by Catholics. O'Connell was at pains to stress that the granting of an Irish parliament would preserve rather than destroy the Union and that the interests of landlords and Protestants would be protected along with improving the lives of the Catholic peasants. There was something for everyone!

Some historians have even doubted whether his commitment to Repeal was genuine at all. Given the determined opposition of the government and the denunciation of violence, there was little real prospect of the campaign achieving success. Perhaps it was merely a tactic to squeeze more fundamental changes for Ireland within the Union.

◢ Source

Why, then, repeal? The answer is, I think, that O'Connell did not intend it as a specific proposition or demand. It was rather, in lawyer's language, an invitation to treat, an attempt to elicit a proposition from the British government.

> Quoted in Oliver Macdonagh, **States of Mind – Two centuries of Anglo-Irish conflict, 1780–1980** (Allen and Unwin, 1983)

Whatever his intentions, O'Connell's tactics were clear and dramatic. He intended to mobilise the masses in order to put pressure on the government. He was helped in this by the launch of a new newspaper, *The Nation*, edited by a group of middle-class young men including

Thomas Davis, John Blake Dillon and Charles Gavin Duffy. Its aim was to encourage an Irish national identity and was the forerunner of the Gaelic Renaissance associated with the later part of the century. Davis was mainly responsible for the editorials and he tried to stress that Irishness was common to both the native Catholic and the Protestant settler alike. The appeal cut little ice with the latter who were increasingly disturbed by concessions to the Catholic majority and identified their interests with preservation of the Union.

The key feature of the repeal movement, however, was the organisation of 'monster meetings', strictly controlled by O'Connell. By amassing as many as three-quarters of a million people at each outdoor meeting, he believed that the government could not fail to be impressed.

◢ Source

We are at Tara of the Kings – the spot from which emanated the social power, the legal authority, the right to dominion over the furthest extremes of the land ... The strength and majority of the national movement was never exhibited so imposingly as at this great meeting. The numbers exceed any that ever before congregated in Ireland in peace or war ... Step by step we are approaching the great goal of Repeal of the Union, but it is at length with the strides of a giant.

Daniel O'Connell, August 1843, on the Royal Hill of Tara, chosen for its ancient Gaelic tradition (although O'Connell claimed more significance for it than it deserved).
*Quoted in Robert Kee, **Ireland, A History** (Weidenfeld and Nicolson, 1980)*

As it happened, Peel called his bluff and banned the meeting planned for 1843 at Clontarf. Rather than risk possible violence between his supporters and the authorities, O'Connell climbed down and called off the meeting. This marked the effective end of his political career, although he lived until 1847. His alliance with the Young Ireland group of Davis and others was ended. They were frustrated by O'Connell's close association with the Catholic hierarchy which they believed alienated Protestant support. More fundamentally, they broke with O'Connell over political aims and methods. In 1846, they came out in support of the possible use of violence and the setting up of an independent Irish Republic. Neither of these had entered O'Connell's thoughts and they were expelled from the association. They were to attempt that armed rebellion in 1848, only for it to fail, like so many others, through lack of support and organisation. With the onset of famine, the Repeal Association had become irrelevant. Despite dramatic successes in his early career, O'Connell was a failure in the 1840s. He had crumbled in the face of a determined Peel who must have felt sweet revenge for Emancipation. Sadly, even his achievements on behalf of his fellow Catholics deepened the divisions which already existed between Irish Catholics and Protestants.

Peel and Ireland

Sir Robert Peel had a long association with Ireland. He had served his political apprenticeship as Chief Secretary between 1812 and 1818. Then, as Home Secretary in the 1820s, he had had general charge of Irish affairs. His natural instincts were both deeply conservative and Protestant. His stand against Emancipation and support for the Protestant Ascendancy earned for him the nickname 'Orange Peel'. However, he was above all a practical politician and efficient administrator. Although he has been accused of betraying his principles, his changes of mind came about when he realised there was no practical alternative. This was certainly the case with Emancipation in 1829. When he became Prime Minister in 1841, he brought with him both experience of Irish issues and understanding of them.

Of course, as Prime Minister, there were plenty of other issues to occupy his attention. The Repeal campaign forced him to deal with Irish matters once again. He realised that the suppression of the movement was not enough. He was convinced that the educated Catholic community needed to be reconciled to the Union and detached from the mass of Irish peasants. To this end, he proposed the endowment of the Catholic Church, better training facilities for Catholic priests and university education for the Catholic middle classes. This was a bold policy because it was bound to face opposition from Protestants in his own party. His proposal to give a generous state grant to Maynooth College, where Catholic priests were trained, became law in 1845. Almost inevitably, it split the Conservative Party with over half of the Conservative MPs voting against it. Only the support of the Irish and Whig opposition allowed it to become law. Peel established university colleges at Belfast, Cork and Galway but there was Catholic suspicion of the idea of making these non-denominational. The Catholic Church wanted control over the education of its faithful.

In 1843 Peel launched a far-reaching enquiry into conditions in rural Ireland. The Devon Commission reported in 1845, but it was already too late to prevent the disaster of the Famine. His decision to repeal the Corn Laws in 1846 was consistent with his policy of free trade, but the Famine provided the occasion for the crisis. Free trade in corn could not in itself feed the starving peasants, but it would be difficult to justify expecting the British taxpayer to pay for famine relief while there were still restrictions on the import of corn. The crisis ended Peel's political life but it is worth noting that the emergency measures he put into effect ensured that no-one died of starvation during the time he was in office.

In his last years Peel proposed far-reaching reforms for Irish agriculture and the transfer of land to the tenant, but his voice was now a faint cry. Like so many others, he was hindered in office by the realities of practical politics. After all, the Famine had happened despite the hundreds of official reports warning of the dangers in the 40 or so years of the existence of the Union. Was it therefore the fault of the Union itself? By 1850, none of the reforms introduced by successive British governments had provided solutions to the real economic problems of an inadequate land system and lack of industrial development, with the exception of Protestant Ulster. There was still mistrust among Catholics and opposition to the Union. As long as the Anglican Church and Protestant landlord class appeared to be favoured by the link with Britain, this was unlikely to change.

The Famine and its consequences (1845–68)

The tragedy of the Famine lies not in the successive failure of the potato crop between 1845 and 1848. The crop failed all over Europe and there was plenty of other food in Ireland. During one of the worst years of the Famine – 1848 – the following left the port of Cork on a single day:

◢ Source

147 bales of bacon
120 casks and 135 barrels of pork
5 casks of hams
149 casks miscellaneous provisions
1,996 sacks, and 950 barrels of oats
300 bags of flour
300 head of cattle
239 sheep
9,398 firkins of butter
542 boxes of eggs

*Quoted in Robert Kee, **Ireland, A History** (Weidenfeld and Nicolson, 1980)*

The tragedy can only be found in the chaotic land system which left millions of Irish peasants reliant on a single crop without the means to buy alternatives – a system which condemned those peasants to a subsistence on meagre plots of land on which they were forced to scrape a living. It is impossible to avoid two vital questions:

Could the disaster have been prevented?

Did the authorities do enough to deal with the crisis?

Of course it could have been prevented. With the benefit of hindsight and a twentieth-century perspective, we can easily see that a commitment of government expenditure and farsightedness could have transformed Irish agriculture and prevented the Famine. Such an assessment is, however, unhistorical. Governments had to deal with the political realities of the day and what was needed would have amounted to a political, social and economic revolution which was beyond both the will and imagination of the politicians of the day. As far as the other question is concerned, there is a great deal more debate. We have seen that Peel succeeded in preventing deaths as long as he remained in office through the emergency measures he put into effect. The record of the Whig administration needs closer examination.

◢ Source

It is easy ... to look back and say, quite correctly, that the accusations of genocide made by some writers at the time and since were unjust and absurd; that the government was the prisoner of the economic philosophy of the day, which taught that economic laws had a natural operation and that to interfere with them was to breed chaos and anarchy; that far from looking on callously, the government looked on with an increasing sense of dismay at what it regarded as its helplessness before irresistible economic and social forces; that, eventually, by what seemed a superhuman effort at the time, it succeeded in abandoning at least some of the principles it held most sacred and brought itself to distribute government charity, expecting only in return that its recipients should continue to live. All this is true ... The agricultural lower classes of Ireland were of no less theoretical concern to the government than the industrial classes of England. The trouble was simply that in neither case was the concern great enough.

*Quoted in Robert Kee, **The Green Flag – A History of Irish Nationalism** (Weidenfeld and Nicolson, 1972)*

The man charged with the responsibility for dealing with the Famine by the new Whig government in 1846 was Charles Trevelyan. He was not without compassion, but he was firmly wedded to the principles of **laissez-faire**. He believed that to interfere with market forces would do more harm than good. There was no question of feeding the starving at the taxpayers' expense. To him the prime responsibility lay with Irish ratepayers. The workhouses were to provide for the poor while public workschemes would provide much needed employment. They both proved totally inadequate. People were dying in their thousands every day. When the government relented and provided direct help to the starving, Trevelyan concluded that too much had been done for the Irish already. It is difficult to escape the following verdict:

◢ Source

Talk of the power of England, her navy, her gold, her resources – oh yes, and her enlightened statesmen, while the broad fact is manifested that she cannot keep the children of her bosom from perishing by hunger ...

*The Cork Examiner, 1846. Quoted in Robert Kee, **Ireland, A History** (Weidenfeld and Nicolson, 1980)*

KEY TERM

Laissez-faire can be translated as 'leave alone'. This was the belief that the state should not intervene in the nation's economy. It was based on the idea, made popular by Adam Smith in his book *The Wealth of Nations*, that market forces, free from state control, determine a nation's wealth.

The immediate consequences of the Famine show the scale of the disaster. About one million men, women and children died from either starvation or disease; a further one and a half million emigrated to escape death. The population fell by about 25 per cent between 1841 and 1851 and continued its decline. Today the figure is 50 per cent of what it was in the 1840s. It virtually wiped out the class of landless labourers and the smallholders. The terrible truth is that during the height of the Famine, those smallholder tenants were being evicted as they were starving to death. Those carrying out the evictions were just as likely to be Catholics as Protestants who could see the opportunity of effecting clearances and increasing rents on their land.

Ironically, the Famine, by reducing the pressure on the land, created a more balanced farming system. As less land was needed for the potato, the move to more pastoral farming was accelerated. The size of plots generally increased except in the west of Ireland and farmers began to experience greater prosperity, at least until the 1870s. Housing improved as the one-roomed cabins slowly disappeared, towns began to grow in size and more schools were built. For those who survived, the Famine brought unexpected benefits!

Despite the abortive Young Ireland rebellion of 1848, the two decades after the Famine witnessed something of a political lull. The Irish Party disintegrated with the demise of O'Connell and the Conservative Party actually won a majority of Irish seats in 1859. The reasons for this lull are not that surprising. The middling tenant farmers now made up the majority; understandably they were too busy with immediate economic interests to wrestle with the more intellectual pursuits of national politics. They were prepared to campaign, but in the pursuit of their economic interests as tenants rather than for direct political goals. Those who kept alive the Republican spirit of 1848 were few and had to bide their time.

One such Young Ireland veteran was James Stephens. He spent the 1850s learning his revolutionary trade in Paris and travelling around Ireland to gauge the potential for support. Towards the end of the decade he was convinced that the potential existed. What finally persuaded him was a delayed consequence of the Famine. Those forced to emigrate to America took with them a deep hatred of Britain, which they blamed for both the Famine and their leaving their homeland. Many had established a more prosperous and influential life in their adopted home. With the promise of financial backing from these emigrants, Stephens could see the potential of the Atlantic link. He launched the Irish Republican Brotherhood in 1858 and the Fenian Brotherhood in America soon afterwards. By 1865, many potential supporters had experience of military action during the American Civil War. He believed he could count on the support of 85,000 men in Ireland alone. Plans were laid for a rising in both Ireland and Britain, and even against British forces in Canada. Stephens himself lost control of the organisation in 1866, but the Rising was to go ahead under the new command of General Kelly. Like the rising of 1848 it was abortive, but the violence which was brought to England by the Fenians provides the background to the next phase in the development of the Irish Question. In 1868, William Gladstone became the Liberal Prime Minister and announced his 'mission to pacify Ireland'.

This chapter has been concerned with the effectiveness of British rule in Ireland from the Union to 1868. One way of gaining a better understanding of any historical situation is through role-play. It requires the ability to suspend your own personality and, rather like an actor, see the world through the eyes of another character in a different time and place.

Imagine that you are a civil servant in 1868. You have long experience of working for a number of Chief Secretaries for Ireland. You have been asked to prepare a report for William Gladstone, the new Prime Minister. He has declared his intention to pacify the Irish. He wants to know how effective British policy has been since the Union and the grievances felt by Irish people. In addition, he wants some advice about what he needs to do to remove those concerns.

Now, write your report with your recommendations. Take care to keep the interests of *all* Ireland's people in mind. When you read the next chapter you will be able to compare your recommendations with Gladstone's actual Irish policy. Don't be tempted to cheat. Do your report first!

CHAPTER TWO

GLADSTONE AND IRELAND

Objectives

◢ To understand Gladstone's attempts to find solutions to the Irish Question

◢ To assess the reasons for Gladstone's failure to solve the Irish Question.

Parnell's political career coincided closely with that of William Gladstone, leader of the British Liberal Party. Gladstone was Prime Minister on four occasions: 1868–74, 1880–85, 1886 and 1892–94. They were, at different times, both political opponents and allies and their political fortunes were closely linked.

This chapter is concerned with Gladstone's attempts to find solutions to the Irish Question. It provides the context in which Parnell operated. Its main focus is determined by two related issues:

◢ What motivated Gladstone to attempt a constructive policy for Ireland?

◢ Why did Gladstone fail to pacify Ireland?

The first of these is a matter of some debate. The classic view is that Gladstone was a man of vision, motivated by a deep religious conviction and a desire to do good: when he received the news that he was to be Prime Minister in 1868, he is reputed to have said, 'My mission is to pacify Ireland'. These words are often quoted as evidence of a genuine desire to achieve justice for Ireland.

This classic view is closely associated with the historian, J. L. Hammond. In his book, *Gladstone and the Irish Nation*, he argues that Gladstone singlehandedly set out to remove Irish grievances in the belief that this would result in a working relationship between Britain and Ireland. To do this, Gladstone was prepared to confront the religious and racial prejudices of the British establishment and risk his own political career in the pursuit of a greater good.

More recently, historians have tended to revise this view. They point out that the issues facing Gladstone in 1868 were urgent and required attention from whoever was in power. Roy Foster asks quizzically, 'What might Disraeli's mission have been if he had returned to power in 1868?' (*Modern Ireland, 1600–1972*, Allen Lane, 1988).

This view sees Gladstone responding to events and circumstances rather than putting into effect any long-term strategies to remove Irish grievances. In 1867, the Fenian Rising took place and the Second Reform Act was passed. The former involved violent incidents in mainland Britain (see Part One), while the latter increased the size of the electorate in Britain and Ireland to include working-class voters for the first time.

However genuine his desire to do justice to Ireland, there is little doubt that the Fenians made an impact on public opinion that Gladstone made use of. After the passing of the Second Reform Act by his rival, Benjamin Disraeli, he needed to find an issue to unite all Liberals. This must be one of the reasons why Gladstone chose his reform of the Irish Church as the central election issue of 1868. Later, the Land War of 1879–82 and the agricultural depression which preceded it provide the background to the passing of the Second Land Act of 1881. The introduction of the secret ballot in 1872 increased the political independence of Irish tenant farmers. Parnell made use of this and the further extension of the franchise in 1884–85 to mould a tightly disciplined Irish Party in the House of Commons.

After the election of 1885, Parnell's party held the balance of power and could put either of the two main parties in office. Gladstone's famous conversion to Home Rule in 1885–86 must be seen in the light of these political realities.

When Gladstone finally retired from office in 1894, he had failed in his 'mission' to find a permanent solution to the Irish Question. This failure needs to be explained. The following section considers the nature of Gladstone's legislative programme for Ireland. It asks whether the explanation for his failure lies in the programme itself and whether alternatives might have been more successful. It points out the scale of the task and the constraints facing Gladstone in trying to achieve it.

Gladstone's Irish policy

It is possible to see Gladstone's Irish policy as a kind of journey. His first steps are tentative and uncertain. As he becomes more familiar with the nature and the scale of the problem, his measures become more sophisticated and purposeful. His early legislation can be seen as an attempt to reconcile the Irish to the Union. Firstly, by disestablishing the Anglican Church of Ireland, he hoped that the sense of injustice felt by the Catholic majority might be removed. Then, by reforming the land system, Irish tenant farmers might feel more secure in possession of their land and believe they had a stake in the Union. If that failed to content the Irish, might it be necessary to consider giving the Irish people some control over their own affairs?

This interpretation is largely unacceptable. It accepts the myth that Gladstone had a ready-made 'blueprint' for Ireland and fails to acknowledge the range of factors affecting Gladstone's policy towards Ireland at different times. However, there is a thread of consistency running through his policy. He was prepared, more than any other British politician of his generation, to be constructive and respond to his perception of Irish needs and wishes. While others retreated into deeply felt and traditional suspicion and prejudice, Gladstone was bold in his efforts to see the issues through Irish eyes.

The Irish Church Act 1869

Gladstone fought the election of 1868 on the issue of religious equality. It was an appeal to the **Nonconformists** in Britain, the backbone of support for the Liberals. It was not surprising, then, that he should proceed to the disestablishment of the Anglican Church of Ireland almost as soon as he took office. The Church Bill had two main elements: **disestablishment** and **disendowment**.

KEY TERM

Nonconformists: this term was applied to all Protestants who were not members of the Church of England. Alternatively, they were known as 'dissenters'.

The first part meant that the link between Church and State was to be removed and the Church of Ireland would become a self-financing, voluntary organisation from 1 January 1871. Irish people would no longer be compelled to pay the hated tithe and Irish Anglican archbishops and bishops would lose the right to sit in the House of Lords.

Disendowment involved the thorny problem of what to do with the property and assets of the Church of Ireland. The proposals offered £10 million pounds for pensions and compensation to the Anglican clergy for losing their positions and £13 million was set aside for education in Ireland.

Another clause of the bill allowed tenants of Church lands to buy their holdings and as many as 6,000 were to take the opportunity. Although this was on a small scale, it was the beginning of the process of transferring ownership of land to the tillers of the soil; a process which was to accelerate over the next 40 years.

As expected, the Bill passed the House of Commons easily and the House of Lords, so soon after the election, was in no position to challenge it. In effect, it made little difference to the lives of most Irish people. The tithe was abolished but responsibility for collecting it had already passed to the landlords in the 1830s. It did, however, have important political and symbolic significance. It removed the last religious grievance felt by the Catholic majority. More importantly, it represented a constructive response to the feelings of the native people, in contrast to the usual round of Coercion Acts restricting the liberties of Irish people. Its significance was not lost on Gladstone's opponents either. It represented the first breach in the Union. Ireland was being treated differently to the rest of the mainland and recognised as a special case. If its intention was to reconcile the Irish to the Union, there was the danger of having the opposite effect of encouraging the idea of Irish separateness.

The Irish Land Act 1870

Gladstone believed that the religious concession had to be accompanied by a solution to the problem of the land. He seems to have been genuinely optimistic in the belief that the twin measures would provide the final solution to the Irish Question. This optimism, in the light of subsequent events, appears misplaced. However, the Land Act, like the Church Act, had almost revolutionary implications.

The main terms of the Irish Land Act of 1870 included loans of public money to tenants to buy their holdings, limited the power of landlords to evict their tenants and provided courts with a scale of compensation payments to evicted tenants, payable by landlords. Finally, the custom of tenant right in Ulster, providing security of tenure, was recognised in law for the whole of Ireland.

Despite the opposition representing landlord interests, the secure Liberal majority ensured the smooth passage of the Bill through the House of Commons. The Lords, again, were reluctant to seriously challenge it. However, they did secure an important amendment which limited the effectiveness of the Act for the protection of the tenants.

The Act failed to solve the problem of the land. Gladstone hoped that the compensation clauses would deter landlords from unfairly evicting their tenants. The Lords' amendment meant that courts were empowered to revise 'exorbitant' rather than 'excessive' rents. As the courts were dominated by the landlord class, they tended to decide in favour of their own kind. More importantly, the Act failed to address the demands of the Irish Tenant Right Party – the 'three Fs':

- **fair rent** decided by disinterested land courts
- **free sale** of the tenant's interest in the property
- **fixity of tenure** as long as a fair rent was paid.

Irish tenants saw themselves as part-owners of the land. They wanted to be secure against eviction, not be compensated for it. The terms offered to tenants to buy their holdings were unattractive and few were able to take the opportunity. The Irish Land Act ignored the real causes of rural poverty: the lack of economic growth, the need for investment and the shortage of land available for cultivation, especially in the remote West. With the onset of depression in the late 1870s, the Act became irrelevant. Landlords were desperate to limit their losses from declining incomes by evicting their tenants and increasing rents.

However ineffective the economic elements of the Act were, its political significance was far more important. It represented a desire by Gladstone to give a message to Irish people that they could look to the government in Westminster to legislate in their interests. Here was a government prepared to depart from its usual commitment to the principle of *laissez-faire* and intervene on behalf of tenants. Opponents of Gladstone were quick to point out that Irish landlords were no longer free to do as they pleased with their own property. The Land Act was seen as an attack on property and landlords on the mainland feared for their own estates. In fact, Ireland was being treated as a special case – Ireland could no longer be regarded as an integral part of the Union. This had a profound effect on Irish Protestants. The security they had previously felt that their interests were guaranteed by the link with Britain was severely shaken.

◢ Source

In future ... the Protestants will find themselves without any privileges ... The poor Protestants are all very irritated. They never did imagine that England would have abandoned their cause.

Cardinal Cullen, Catholic Archbishop of Ireland, reporting to Rome in 1870.
Quoted in F. S. L. Lyons, **Ireland since the Famine** (Fontana Press, 1971)

Lyons makes the point that Gladstone's Irish legislation represented a fresh way of looking at Irish problems; it marked a new relationship between English Liberalism and Irish Catholicism which threatened the security of the Protestant Ascendancy in Ireland. It highlights a problem which has dogged British administrations ever since. By appearing to favour one side of the sectarian divide, there was the risk of alienating the other. Later, in promoting Home Rule, Gladstone chose to ignore the concerns of the Ulster Unionists on the democratic principle that a minority should not be allowed to overturn the wishes of the overwhelming majority. He failed to recognise that any solution to the Irish Question needed to reconcile the interests of both Catholic and Protestant in Ireland.

The Irish Universities Bill 1873

Gladstone clearly underestimated the strength of *sectarian* feeling in his proposals for university education in Ireland. By 1872, the Liberal government was losing its hold over public opinion and control of parliament. Gladstone's radical policies had aroused opposition and his political opponents felt more confident. When he presented his Irish Universities Bill in the House of Commons in March 1873, it was defeated by three votes. A number of Irish Liberal MPs either abstained or voted against the measure. The defeat led to Gladstone's resignation and the disunity within the Liberal Party contributed to its election defeat in 1874.

KEY TERM

Sectarian means divided by religion or belief. This term is usually applied to the religious divide between Protestants and Catholics in Ireland.

Gladstone's proposal to establish a non-denominational University of Dublin for both Catholics and Protestants was designed to increase tolerance and understanding across the sectarian divide. Instead, the measure failed because of intolerance and distrust. Catholics and Protestants preferred their own colleges.

By the time Gladstone returned to power in 1880, there had been significant developments in the Irish Question which he was forced to confront. His Irish policies in the 1880s did not represent the resumption of unfinished business. He resigned the leadership in 1875 after the Liberal defeat and there were no plans in 1880 for further Irish reform. His programme, however, had clearly failed to solve the Irish Question: the emergence of a more robust Nationalist movement under the leadership of Parnell and the onset of social unrest in the late 1870s over the land issue were evidence of his failure. The Irish were far from pacified.

The Second Land Act 1881

The General Election of 1880 was not fought over Irish issues. Gladstone had emerged from his retirement in 1875 to attack Disraeli's foreign and imperial policy. The dominant role he played in the election campaign made him leader and Prime Minister for the second time. He later admitted that he was unaware of the crisis looming in Ireland. The Land Act of 1881 was therefore a response to the immediate crisis in Ireland.

Gladstone was confronted by the Land War orchestrated by the Land League, under the leadership of Michael Davitt and Parnell himself (see Part One and Chapter 3). However, there were warning signs for Gladstone as early as 1874. Support for the Liberals in Ireland was on the decline. Isaac Butt's Home Rule League won 59 seats to the Liberals'

12 in 1874. In 1868, the Liberals had won 66 Irish seats. Despite the weakness and loose organisation of Butt's party, the result of 1874 represented a rejection of the Union as it operated and an indication that Gladstone had failed to find a permanent solution.

Between 1877 and 1880, Charles Parnell emerged as Butt's successor and transformed the Irish Party into a disciplined political force. The link between the issues of Nationalism and the Land was forged in 1879 when the Irish National Land League was formed with Parnell as President. This was further strengthened by the moral and financial support given by Irish Americans.

The violence generated by the Land War, directed against landlords and those who cooperated with the authorities, was the major factor in the crisis facing Gladstone in 1880. Agricultural depression set in after 1877 and conflict between landlords and tenants renewed as evictions increased in an effort by landowners to protect their incomes – the spectre of Famine once again haunted the land. The Land League, while officially denouncing violence, was determined to protect the interests of the tenants and resist evictions. Their activities represented a national, widespread and alternative authority to British rule; their unofficial land courts were successful in securing rent reductions from landlords. The new British government faced the prospect of social revolution in Ireland.

At first, Gladstone reluctantly agreed to respond in the traditional manner – a new Coercion Act was passed early in 1881 giving increased powers of arrest and imprisonment to the authorities. However, Gladstone realised that the crisis could not be resolved by force alone. His second Land Act was primarily political and, as such, was ultimately successful. By granting the 'three Fs' – the main plank of the Land League's demands – he cut the ground from under the organisation and placed Parnell in a difficult position. Parnell realised that tenants would rush to the new land courts to secure legally recognised rent reductions. His advice to tenants to 'test the Act' was a desperate attempt to maintain the support of both militant and moderate opinion in Ireland and the USA.

By October 1881, Gladstone appeared to have 'trumped' Parnell and the Land League only to play into Parnell's hands. Using the powers of the Coercion Act, Gladstone authorised the arrest and imprisonment of the leaders, including Parnell himself. This was really a response to Parnell's refusal to cooperate over the Land Act. His imprisonment had the effect of consolidating support for Parnell at the very moment when it was in danger of breaking up. The Land League was outlawed and the level of violence increased. Gladstone was forced to conclude that only Parnell could control the situation in Ireland. For his part, Parnell realised that the crisis on the land was over and there was more to be gained from an accommodation with the Liberal government.

The unofficial 'Kilmainham Treaty' of April 1882 secured Parnell's release. Under its terms, Gladstone agreed to relax the coercion measures and include in the operation of the Land Act those in arrears of rent. In return, Parnell agreed to use his influence to control the violence and encourage cooperation over the Land Act.

The Land Act can be criticised on economic grounds:

◢ Source

The impact on Irish agriculture appears to be negligible. It did nothing to solve the problems of the smallholders in the west whose land hunger [was unsatisfied] ... Since most tenants already enjoyed the traditional rights of free sale and fixity of tenure, the legalisation of such customs made little difference.

From M. Winstanley, ***Ireland and the Land Question (1800–1922)*** *(Methuen, Lancaster Pamphlets, 1984)*

Rather than provide incentives to improve agricultural efficiency, the Act simply had the consequence of reducing rents by about 20 per cent. Landlords were demoralised by the lack of control over their estates and showed that they were increasingly ready to sell. This was only delayed because the tenants were given no real incentive to buy. Later, Conservative measures improved the terms on offer.

However, as the motives behind the Act were political rather than economic, it should be judged accordingly. In some ways, Gladstone's policy can be viewed as a success. It encouraged the majority of Irish peasants to cooperate with the legitimate authority of the British government and averted the threat of social revolution. It helped to confirm Parnell's view that greater emphasis should be placed on a constitutional, rather than a revolutionary, approach. By replacing the Land League with the National League, he shifted the emphasis onto the national rather than the agrarian issue. Cooperation, rather than conflict, with the British government seemed to offer the best hope of progress for Nationalist aspirations. This can be seen as a failure of Gladstone's policy. The events of 1879–82 had not reconciled the Irish to the Union and Nationalist candidates continued to do well in elections at the expense of the Liberals. Ominously, by 1885, Irish voters were choosing between Unionists and Home Rulers. In Britain, the Land Act was viewed as a further attack on the rights of property. 'Frightened property' increasingly looked to the Conservative Party to protect their interests and there was clearly a drift of support among the propertied classes away from the Liberals. Gladstone's Irish policy was an important factor in the decline of the Liberal Party.

Home Rule (1885–86)

The demand for some form of self-government was a political reality which British politicians in general, not only Gladstone, were forced to confront during this period. After 1882, Parnell moulded popular opinion in Ireland through the National League into an expression of the demand for Home Rule. The League gave the Irish Party an effective organisation at local level to sponsor and support candidates. It was helped in this by the extension of the franchise in the Third Reform Act of 1884–85 to the agricultural labourer. Parnell had an almost autocratic hold over nationalist opinion in Ireland and over his colleagues in the Irish Party. He was further strengthened by the support given to him by the Irish Catholic Church, which came out openly in favour of Home Rule. He could rely on the discipline of the party to act as a single body.

British politicians realised that Parnell's party was now in a position to determine the outcome of a general election. By holding the balance of power, Parnell could put either the Liberals or Conservatives in office. Conservatives, like Lord Randolph Churchill, were quick to flirt with the Irish Party and suggest that they had more to offer Parnell than the Liberals could. Parnell was keen to assert the independence of his party from the Liberals and advised Irishmen living in Britain to vote

Conservative in the election of 1885. The result of the election was one of the most remarkable in British history: the Liberal majority of 86 was exactly equalled by the return of 86 Irish Home Rulers (335 Liberals; 249 Conservatives).

When parliament re-assembled in December 1885, Parnell sided with the Conservatives and kept them in office. It now appears that Gladstone had decided that Home Rule was inevitable. He deliberately kept quiet in the belief that the measure would be introduced by the Conservatives. If so, the Conservatives were in a better position to overcome opposition in both houses of parliament. On the other hand, Gladstone realised that if he publicly supported the measure, he ran the risk of splitting the Liberal Party. However, it soon became obvious that Lord Salisbury and the Conservatives were not prepared to go as far as advocating Home Rule. They could see the potential of patriotic opposition to Home Rule on the principle of maintaining the integrity of the Empire. It would give them a new political identity and advance their political fortunes.

Gladstone's son, Herbert, was afraid that Joseph Chamberlain planned to take over the leadership of the Liberal Party and redirect it towards radical social reform. He calculated that no time could be lost and the Irish needed to be persuaded to switch support to the Liberals. He therefore leaked the news of his father's conversion to Home Rule to the press on 17 December 1885. Immediately, the Irish lined up against the Conservative government and forced its resignation. Gladstone became Prime Minister for the third time in January 1886.

The introduction of Home Rule in April 1886 proved disastrous for both Gladstone and the Liberal Party. Any hope that it would lead to a permanent solution to the Irish Question was misplaced. The Home Rule Bill was defeated in the House of Commons by 30 votes; 93 Liberals voted against it. (The reasons for its failure are complex and are considered later in this chapter.) The dissolution of Parliament which followed made Home Rule the election issue. The result of the election of 1886 was a clear victory for the opponents of Home Rule; the coalition of Conservatives and Liberal Unionists won 394 seats to the Liberals' 191. Gladstone had not only failed to carry Home Rule, but the Liberal Party was condemned to opposition for the best part of the next two decades. For their part, the Conservatives and Unionists were committed to defence of the Union and 'resolute government' of Ireland.

The Second Home Rule Bill 1893

Despite his defeat, Gladstone remained firmly wedded to Home Rule as Liberal Party policy as the permanent solution to the Irish Question. He was presented with one last opportunity in 1892 when the Liberals secured an election victory with Irish support. As expected, Gladstone presented a new Home Rule bill to the House of Commons. This time it passed the House of Commons by 43 votes but was rejected in the Lords by the massive margin of 419 votes to 41. The Liberal Cabinet was not inclined to take on the House of Lords in a constitutional battle over Home Rule despite Gladstone's wishes. His colleagues judged that the British electorate had shown no enthusiasm for Home Rule. Increasingly isolated, Gladstone chose the occasion of a dispute over naval expenditure to resign the leadership in March 1894.

Gladstone had clearly failed in his 'mission to pacify Ireland' – the issue of the land was unresolved and the national demand unsatisfied. Before explaining why he failed, it is worth considering whether the Conservative and Unionist policy, pursued after the Home Rule crisis of 1885–86, had any greater chance of success. The basic tenet of the policy was to deny the nationalist demand altogether. Instead, they adopted a policy which combined a firm commitment to upholding the rule of law with a programme of economic investment and transfer of land to the peasants. Was it possible to find a solution to the Irish Question within the Union and 'kill Home Rule with kindness'? Could Irishmen, of whatever persuasion and tradition, be convinced that their interests were best served by being part of the United Kingdom? Had, after all, Gladstone misjudged the situation by presuming that only Home Rule could provide the basis for a permanent settlement?

Constructive Unionism

This term is used by F. S. L. Lyons in his book *Ireland since the Famine* to describe the positive attempts made by the Conservatives and

Unionists to find solutions to the Irish Question between 1886 and 1905. It represents the other side of Lord Salisbury's promise to provide 'resolute government' of Ireland. This tough policy followed the traditional line of coercion. In response to the Plan of Campaign organised by William O'Brien and John Dillon to resist evictions, rather as the Land League had done, a new Crimes Act was passed in 1887. It was rigorously applied by the new Chief Secretary for Ireland, Arthur Balfour, Lord Salisbury's nephew. He was determined to imprison anyone who broke the law. In one incident, in Michelstown, the police shot dead three of a crowd protesting against eviction. As a result, Balfour earned the nickname 'Bloody Balfour'. Any constructive plans for Ireland would have to wait.

Despite the fact that Parnell now distanced himself from agrarian protests, the solid group of over 80 Irish Nationalists remained an uncomfortable presence in the House of Commons for the Conservative and Unionist alliance. It was clearly in their interest to discredit Parnell. *The Times* launched its 'Parnellism and Crime' campaign in April 1887 (see Part One and Chapter 4). As it turned out, the campaign against him failed and Parnell was cleared of any involvement in the Phoenix Park murders of 1882. Instead, Parnell was given a standing ovation in the Commons in 1889 and was hailed as the 'uncrowned King of Ireland'.

The scandal of the O'Shea affair (see Part One and Chapter 5) destroyed Parnell's career just before his death and it was this which gave the Conservatives the opportunity they were waiting for. The affair split the Nationalists into pro-Parnellites and anti-Parnellites and weakened the Nationalist movement. Balfour could now begin to build the programme of Constructive Unionism.

This consisted of a number of different elements. One of these was to extend the land purchase schemes begun by Gladstone as early as 1869. Financial help to peasants had been provided by Lord Ashbourne's Act in 1885. Now, in 1891, the Land Purchase Act extended the scheme. However, the terms were not attractive enough to persuade sufficient numbers to buy. Not until Wyndham's Act of 1903 was there the incentive to buy at the time when landlords were keen to sell. Tenants were then offered government loans at the low rate of interest of 3.25 per cent repayable over 68 years. By 1920, the transfer of land to those who worked it was almost complete.

The particular problems affecting the people living in the West of Ireland were at last confronted by the Congested Districts Board, set up in 1891. It provided subsidies for local industries and gave technical instruction, encouraged larger holdings and land purchase and helped to improve the quality of agriculture in the worst areas. By 1912, it had over £500,000 to dispense. The problem of underemployment was tackled through public works schemes: roads and bridges were built, as well as light railways.

The changes during this period amounted to something like a quiet revolution. Much of the credit is due to Sir Horace Plunkett and his Recess Committee. Their advice and services offered to the Department of Agriculture were largely responsible for the general improvement in the quality of farming during this period. The Local Government Act of 1898 revolutionised local politics; its largely democratic franchise was far-reaching and meant that power and influence moved away from the landlord class and into the hands of farmers, shopkeepers and publicans.

Balfour believed that the Irish Question was really a 'knife and fork question'. The Irish, he calculated, would be satisfied and reconciled to the Union if they could feel real material benefits arising from the Union. In that, he was mistaken. The causes of poverty were slowly being removed, but the nationalist sentiment was very much alive. Although Irish politics were comparatively calm in the last decade of the century, nationalism expressed itself in a cultural form. The Gaelic Renaissance encouraged a self-confident and separate Irish identity through the offices of the Gaelic League and the Gaelic Athletic Association. It represented a deliberate rejection of Anglo-Saxon influence in Ireland.

◢ **Source**

It is the curious certainty that come what may Irishmen will continue to resist English rule, even though it should be for their own good, which prevents many from becoming Unionists upon the spot. It is a fact, and we must face it as a fact, that although they adopt English habits and copy England in every way, the great bulk of Irishmen and

Irishwomen over the whole world are known to be filled with a dull, ever-abiding animosity against her, and – right or wrong – to grieve when she prospers, and joy when she is hurt . . .

Douglas Hyde's presidential address to the National Literary Society, 1892. Quoted in R. F. Foster, **Paddy and Mr Punch** (Allen Lane, 1993)

Gladstone's failure to pacify Ireland

In the period after Parnell's death and Gladstone's fall, the issue of Home Rule may have been dormant, but not dead. We can conclude that Gladstone's judgement was correct. If Ireland was to be pacified, the nationalist demand had to be met. Why, then, did he fail?

The explanation involves a wide range of related factors, but the crude point is that the opposition to Gladstone within the political establishment was too strong to overcome. In 1885–86, not only was the whole of the Conservative Party opposed to Home Rule, but significant sections of his own party were also. This Liberal Unionism is associated with the personalities of Lord Hartington and Joseph Chamberlain. In particular, the motives of Chamberlain have been analysed closely. There are clearly personal reasons for his opposition, including a desire to wrest the leadership of the Liberal Party from Gladstone and steer it onto a more radical course. However, there is also a genuine commitment to the idea of Empire – Chamberlain feared that Home Rule would lead to demands for separation and signal the disintegration of the Empire.

Gladstone has been criticised for not consulting with his party and trying to educate it to accept Home Rule. However, it is difficult to see how this would have made any difference. After all, he believed that the measure stood more chance of success if it was introduced by the Conservatives. Given the opposition within his own party, his tactics demanded that he kept silent. Once it became obvious that the Conservative government was not prepared to go as far as Home Rule, there was no alternative to making public his conversion to the idea.

Parnell has been criticised for encouraging the Irish in Britain to vote Conservative in 1885. It has been calculated that he gave the Conservatives between 25 and 40 seats, enough to have secured a majority for Home Rule in the House of Commons, despite the opposition of the Liberal Unionists. However, as the experience of the 1892 bill shows, the measure would surely have been rejected by the House of Lords. The 1886 election shows the level of anti-Irish feeling which could be stirred up on the mainland. Deep-rooted racial and religious prejudice was clearly a factor in Gladstone's failure to achieve Home Rule. There was a strong feeling in Britain that the Irish could not be trusted to rule themselves and they did not deserve the opportunity.

It is tempting to see the failure of the two Home Rule bills as lost opportunities. Home Rule seemed to offer the best hope of providing a permanent solution to the Irish Question. However, this view is misleading. The implementation of Home Rule would have been beset with difficulties, not least of which was the determined opposition of the Ulster Unionists. Lord Randolph Churchill may have stirred up this opposition in 1886 by 'playing the Orange Card', but it was real enough anyway. There is no reason to believe that the determination to resist Home Rule in 1912 would have been any less in 1886 or 1893. There could be no permanent solution of the Irish Question without an accommodation with the Ulster Unionists. This was as true then as it is now.

It is also unclear whether Home Rule would have been enough to satisfy nationalist aspirations; there were certainly those in the Fenian tradition who wished to go much further. It is undoubtedly true that Gladstone failed because the opposition was too strong. It is equally the case that he may have been attempting the impossible and that there was no solution to the Irish Question capable of satisfying both Nationalists and Unionists in Ireland. This appears to be borne out by the experience of the twentieth century. The historical legacy was such that the Irish Question, the relationship between Britain and Ireland, could never be completely solved.

What are examiners looking for in a good history essay?

Here are some general points, followed by an example taken from the material covered in this chapter in order to illustrate them.

◢ *A relevant answer which directly answers the question*

This may seem obvious but examiners often report that many candidates produce irrelevant and undirected answers. They either have ready-made answers prepared regardless of what the question is or treat each question as if it were, 'write everything you know about ...'. A useful idea is to underline the key words in the question to focus your mind on the issues raised by the question.

◢ *A planned answer which provides a clear structure and a line of argument*

As with a journey, you must know where you are going before you set out! Firstly, decide your direct answer to the question. This provides the basis for your conclusion. You then need to work out your plan of how you are to arrive at your conclusion. Your plan should then consist of brief jottings of the main issues raised by the question, not the detailed content. The plan then becomes the basis for your introduction. The introduction should direct the reader to the main issues to be discussed in the body of the answer in a logical order.

◢ *An answer supported by precise and accurate evidence*

You would not be impressed as a member of a jury with a prosecuting counsel who asked you to find someone guilty without providing the evidence against him or her. So, an examiner cannot give high marks for an answer which provides vague, unsupported assertions.

You must provide precise and accurate evidence, not to show off your knowledge, but to **support your line of argument**.
Example: Why did Gladstone fail to pacify Ireland?
Direct response: there was too much opposition to his measures in both Britain and Ireland.

TASK

Plan
- the grievances felt by the catholic majority; religious, economic and political
- appropriateness of Gladstone's measures; Church Act, land reform, Home Rule
- appropriateness of Conservative alternatives
- Irish response to Gladstone's measures
- determined opposition of Ulster Unionists to Home Rule
- opposition in Britain to Home Rule; Conservatives, Liberal unionists (Hartington and Chamberlain), House of Lords, the electorate
- Gladstone's tactics.

CHAPTER THREE

WHAT KIND OF A NATIONALIST WAS PARNELL?

Objectives
◢ To understand Parnell's political aims and objectives
◢ To consider public opinion in Ireland and America
◢ To analyse the impact on British politics of the Irish Parliamentary Party
◢ To understand that the nature of the evidence can lead historians to different interpretations of Parnell's politics.

The aim of this chapter is to attempt to define Parnell's political philosophy. This is no easy task. Parnell left few personal records except the letters he wrote to Katharine O'Shea, and these provide few insights into his political views. Historians have, therefore, to interpret his public statements and judge his actions in an effort to tease out what he stood for.

This is made more difficult by the fact that his statements appear to be so contradictory. Consider, for instance, these statements made at different times:

◢ Source A

When we have undermined English misgovernment, we have paved the way for Ireland to take her place among the nations of the earth. And let us not forget that is the ultimate goal at which all we Irishmen aim ... None of us, whether we are in America or Ireland, or wherever we may be, will be satisfied until we have destroyed the last link which keeps Ireland bound to England.

Parnell speaking in the USA in 1880

◢ Source B

No man has the right to fix the boundary to the march of a nation. No man has the right to say to his country: thus far shalt thou go and no further. We have never attempted to fix the 'ne plus ultra' to the progress of Ireland's nationhood and we never shall.

Part of a speech made by Parnell in Cork in 1885.
These words are now inscribed on his tomb.

And yet when he spoke in favour of the Home Rule bill in 1886, he said:

◢ Source C

We look upon the provisions of this bill as a final settlement of the Irish Question and I believe that the Irish people have accepted it as a settlement... Not a single dissentient voice has been raised against this bill by any Irishman holding national opinions.

Parnell speaking in the House of Commons during the Home Rule debate, 1886

Such an acceptance would amount to a very limited amount of domestic freedom for Ireland. So, we need to explain these contradictions if we are to get a satisfactory definition of Parnell's nationalism. In fact, any attempt to define Parnell as a politician must begin with asking the right questions:

◢ Was he a constitutional statesman or a revolutionary leader?
◢ Was his ultimate aim the complete separation of Ireland from Great Britain or would he have been content with Home Rule along the lines of the bill of 1886?
◢ Would he have preferred an Ireland run by Irish landowners like himself or was he in favour of a democratic republic?

Finding satisfactory answers to these questions requires an understanding of the political context he was working in, an appreciation of his personality and what motivated him. As Irish leader, he wanted to be effective. He realised that he needed the base of mass support in Ireland itself, the financial and moral support of Irish Americans and a united and disciplined Irish party in the House of Commons. Sustaining his leadership in these circumstances was beset with difficulties. He had to try to keep together different forces, often pulling in different directions. Equally, needs and circumstances change over time and he had to make decisions based on his judgement of the changing situation.

Before considering in detail the phases of his political career and how these affected his Irish nationalism, it is important to set out the main forces acting upon him. In doing so, it is possible to see that Parnell was no free agent capable of directing policy at will. He had to acknowledge these forces and use his political judgement to decide the most appropriate tactics to employ. The main forces, therefore, were:

- public opinion in Ireland
- the American connection
- the Irish Parliamentary Party.

Public opinion in Ireland

It is too simple to divide the Irish people into Catholic and Protestant or Nationalist and Unionist. There were many different interest groups within the Catholic majority and their aims and ideals had the potential to conflict. The most numerous group, the tenant farmers and labourers, tended to pull in a radical direction. They had more faith in direct action to protect their interests on the land. There were, however, smaller but powerful groups which tended towards conservatism and preferred to work within the constitution. These included the electorate of landlords and urban middle class on a restricted franchise before 1885, the media, characterised by the influential *Freeman's Journal*, and the Catholic Church. While there were radicals among the parish priests, the Catholic hierarchy of bishops and archbishops exerted a powerful conservative influence. They were also subject to the influence of the Pope and cardinals in Rome.

All these forces agreed that there should be some degree of freedom from English control, but this was the minimum of agreement and Parnell was constrained by it.

The American connection

Even before the Famine there had been a steady flow of emigration from Ireland. Between 1815 and 1845, at least one million people had left. Between 1845 and 1870 a further three million emigrated. It has been estimated that, by 1890, more than three million people born in Ireland, 40 per cent of the population, were living abroad.

Destinations varied over time but, in the last quarter of the nineteenth century, the vast majority headed for the United States, perhaps as many as 84 per cent of all emigrants. This compares with 7 per cent to Australia and 8 per cent to the United Kingdom. Although experiences varied, in America there appears to have been a distinct Irish-American culture. This included a commitment to the 'old country' left behind. Whatever the truth of the matter, most felt that they had been forced out to escape poverty and starvation. The blame was firmly put on Britain and there was a strong degree of anti-British hatred. This bred a radical republican form of Irish nationalism in America, represented by organisations like the Fenians, Clan na Gael and the National League of America.

Many Irish immigrants had prospered in their adopted home. They were initially attracted to the cities because of the availability of work in the mines and factories. By the end of the nineteenth century, they were increasingly police officers, nurses and civil servants. They were influential in the Catholic Church and made good use of the Catholic educational system. There was a sprinkling of millionaires involved in big business in their number.

Irish Americans were therefore an important source of financial aid for Irish organisations. Large donations were made to the Land League from 1879. Parnell was quick to exploit his American ancestry and made a number of fund-raising tours to the USA. As an astute politician, he was aware of the more extreme flavour of radical republicanism among his American audiences.

The Irish Parliamentary Party

If Parnell was pulled in a radical direction by Irish world opinion, the Irish Parliamentary Party at Westminster was a constraining force. There were radical elements within the parliamentary group like Joseph Biggar and John Barry, both of whom had been members of the Supreme Council of the Irish Republican Brotherhood, and ex-Fenians like John Dillon and J. J. O'Kelly. However, they were exceptions and the Party was dominated, before 1885, by wealthy and successful men from the landed classes and the higher professions. Parnell was himself, of course, an Irish landlord. In an age when there was still deference to social superiors, this was an advantage. Parnell could present himself as the social equal to his British rivals.

Furthermore, the costs involved in getting elected, travelling to London and paying for lodgings and so on, when MPs were still unpaid, were prohibitive. There was some support provided through the resources of the Land League and American donations. Parnell relied heavily on the tribute which was raised among supporters in Ireland. However, most MPs had to be of independent means to sustain themselves.

Until 1885, Irish MPs were elected on a very restricted franchise, by a far wealthier class than in Britain as a whole. An Irish voter in the boroughs needed to own property worth £4 a year, whereas in Britain a voter simply needed to be a householder to qualify. Consequently, Dublin, a city the size of Leeds, had one-quarter of the number of voters. The Irish electorate, therefore, tended to be to the right of public opinion as a whole.

Another conservative force was the political influence of the Catholic Church. Until Parnell was able after 1882 to establish a more independent party machine through the National League, the local clergy provided constituency organisation. Those nominated to stand were often proposed and supported by meetings of the local bishop and priests.

Finally, there was the constraining effect of Westminster itself. Despite the tactics of obstruction and occasional threats to secede from parliament altogether, the Irish Party was part of the House of Commons, an elite club. It is no wonder, then, that the Party generally represented a conservative force, one which favoured a constitutional and pragmatic approach rather than a confrontational and revolutionary one.

Parnell had to balance these often conflicting forces, but they did not stand still. As the circumstances changed, the balance shifted to test Parnell's political skill. It is possible to identify a number of key phases in Parnell's career as Irish leader and chart the different emphases placed on the nature of his commitment to Irish nationalism.

'The New Departure' (1879–82)

During the period 1879 to 1882 Parnell was establishing his position as Irish leader. He needed to be accepted as the spokesman of Irish public opinion and recognised as such by Irish Americans. Equally, he needed to be seen as the undisputed leader of the Irish Party in parliament. In 1879, he was just beginning this process and his chances of success were far from guaranteed. When the opportunity came, he decided that the priority was to be associated with a popular movement at home. He could then court the favour of Irish Americans and assert his claims to the leadership of the parliamentary party. In fact, the idea of uniting pressure on the land with both the revolutionary and constitutional elements of Irish nationalism found favour with Irish Americans. The phrase 'The New Departure' was coined to describe it.

The opportunity was provided by Michael Davitt who invited Parnell, in June 1879, to speak to a group of tenants. Davitt had set up the Land League to resist eviction by landlords and prevent a repeat of the disaster of the Famine. Parnell accepted the invitation and soon became President of the Land League. He had taken a calculated risk because of the danger of alienating the more conservative forces. In fact, he had been advised by the Archbishop of Tuam not to accept the invitation. It is now clear that he supported the League because it represented the interests of the majority of his countrymen at the time and appealed to the anti-landlord, anti-British prejudices of Irish Americans. As the leader of a popular movement, he could secure his own popularity and power. The tactic paid off and his support was duly increased after the general election of 1880. Soon after, he was elected leader of the party.

As his priority was to secure a firm popular base, it is understandable that his speeches and actions at this time were directed at the more radical nationalist elements, both in America and Ireland. However, he could not afford to alienate the more conservative forces by being associated with any violence carried out by the more enthusiastic supporters of the Land League. His tactic was to offer the alternative of 'aggressive moral force', which became known as the 'boycott' (see Key Terms in Part One and the illustrations in this chapter).

The Land War had the potential to become the focus for a social revolution. Michael Davitt wanted land transferred from the owners to the tenants and, ultimately, land nationalisation. As Parnell's sister makes clear in her book on the Land League, Anna felt betrayed by the dropping of the agitation on the land. She calls the Land League 'The Great Sham' because she saw the land war as a phase in the struggle for Irish independence. While her brother and the other leaders were imprisoned in Kilmainham Jail, she took over the running of the organisation through the Ladies Land League. She argues that they could have won the land war and used the pressure to lever the British into accepting Home Rule as a step towards complete independence. When Parnell agreed to the 'Kilmainham Treaty' in April 1882 and disbanded the Land League, she felt personally and politically betrayed.

In an article on 'Anna Parnell and the Land League', Professor T. W. Moody argues that her judgement was faulty and her brother's astute. Charles Parnell judged that the terms of Gladstone's Land Act of 1881 were too tempting to the tenantry to sustain the agitation and that the resources of the Land League were draining away. Far better then to channel the energies of the popular movement towards the constitutional track. By building a strong group in parliament, he believed he could achieve Home Rule. This suggests he was more comfortable as a constitutional leader than as a land agitator and believed he could be more effective in this role. The Land War had served its purpose.

Figures 6–9 (pages 71–74)   These artists' impressions were printed in 1882 in *The Graphic*, an illustrated weekly British newspaper. They were used to illustrate the activities of the Land League and the consequences of boycotting. Even if these events actually occurred, these illustrations represent propaganda in favour of the landlords and the British establishment. Note the sinister portrayal of the 'Landleaguers' compared with the 'innocent' victims.

The Constitutional Approach (1882–85)

◢ Source

Mr Parnell wishes … that the movement in Ireland should be conducted on moderate lines 'til the present coercion act is exhausted. It may be that this is the wisest policy. He believes that after the next election his power in parliament to resist coercion will be increased ten-fold. There can be no doubt that this will be so. He prefers for the next year the Irish race should devote itself to organisation and preparation and that the final step in advance should not be made 'til after the next election.

John Dillon to an American audience in 1883

Figure 6 'This outrage was not, we think, reported in any of the newspapers. It took place in the mountains of Bilbo, Co. Limerick, on the property of Mr O'Grady, who described it to our artist. Mr O'Grady had evicted some tenants, and had police and "emergency men" put into their houses. Being a lonely district, and as no one about the place would supply them with anything, they kept some goats to get milk from. One night in the last week of November the goats were slaughtered by midnight raiders, who cut their heads clean off, and otherwise brutally mauled them.'

Figure 7 'On the last day of the old year a brutal murder was committed in broad daylight at Irishtown, about a mile from Mullingar. About half-past eight o'clock a man wearing a mask entered a house occupied by an aged widow named Anne Croughan and her two daughters, Esther and Anne, and, without uttering a word, presented a revolver at Mrs Croughan, and fired, but the bullet missed its mark. The woman and her daughter, Esther, then ran into a room and bolted the door, but it was broken open by the murderer, who fired four shots in succession at Esther, killing her instantly. Mrs Croughan escaped by getting under a bed, but the murderer then went into another room, where the other daughter lay ill in bed, and fired shots at her, which took effect in the shoulder. He then decamped. The Croughans' only man-servant was away delivering milk at the workhouse, but upon his return immediate information was given to the police, who with several magistrates were quickly on the spot. No clue has yet been obtained as to the murderer.'

Figure 8 'On Nov. 25, a gang of about twenty men, with blackened faces, broke into a cabin at Scrahan, near Listowel, Co. Kerry, occupied by a woman named Bridget Lenane and her three children, who were startled out of their sleep by the bursting in of the door. One of the party struck a light, and the leader saying to the woman, "You have to pay now for acting the informer," pointed his gun at her head; but at that moment one of the children, a boy aged twelve, sprang in front of her, crying out, "I know you, and if you harm my mother you will suffer for it." The weapon was, however, discharged, and though the woman escaped, her little girl, aged seven, was wounded in both legs. Before leaving, the ruffians threatened to shoot the woman dead if she said anything about the outrage. Eight men were subsequently arrested and, being identified by Bridget Lenane, were all committed for trial.'

Figure 9 'A malignant form of "boycotting"was exhibited in November at Baltinglass, Co. Wicklow, where the undertakers refused to supply a hearse to convey the remains of Mr Fenton, a "boycotted" farmer, to the grave. Mr Fitzwilliam Dick sent a carriage from Hemwood to the funeral, and an escort of constabulary had to accompany the *cortege*. A similar scene has taken place more recently, at Mill Street, Co. Cork, where the police had to bury a woman who had dealt with a "boycotted" shopkeeper.'

As these words (page 70) were spoken in America by someone who preferred a more radical approach, they provide evidence of Parnell's increasing authority over the various strands of the nationalist movement. There is no doubt that by committing himself to the constitutional approach and abandoning agitation, he had made a decided shift to the right. There can also be no doubt that the tactics outlined by Dillon were Parnell's genuine priorities. He set up the National League to replace the Land League in October 1882. Its task was electoral organisation in the constituencies with the aim of getting candidates loyal to Parnell elected.

Although Parnell was leader of the Irish Party in 1882, he could rely on the support of only about 30 of the 61 MPs. The immediate concern was not an active policy at Westminster. New rules on the closure of debate meant that 'obstruction' could no longer be as effective. The key was to build a disciplined and united party under Parnell's firm leadership. The party could then assert its independence of either main British party and await the day when the Irish Party could hold the balance between them. When that day came, the Irish would be in a strong negotiating position.

The focus switched to the constituencies of Ireland. The National League deployed local officials to endorse prospective candidates and encourage the idea of party discipline. The work was largely carried out by county conventions representing local feeling but the personal influence of Parnell in deciding who was nominated was strongly felt. The Catholic hierarchy was forced to acknowledge the new situation. Local clergy cooperated with party officials in the nomination process despite an order from the Pope in 1882 not to associate with the National League. In 1884, the Catholic hierarchy urged the party to pursue the claims of Catholic education in parliament. This was a real breakthrough; in 1879–80, Catholic bishops had looked on Parnellites as dangerously subversive.

As the general election approached, the success of the tactics were clear. In 16 by-elections between 1882 and 1885, 15 Parnellites were returned. The old Whig elements were gradually being purged. Most observers agreed that Parnell could have as many as 80 supporters in parliament after the election. The more radical elements had no alternative strategy and were kept in line. So confident was the Parnellite group that in 1884 candidates were pledged to support majority rule in the Party. In effect, this meant obedience to Parnell in the interests of discipline.

Parnell had been helped to sustain his popular support by British attempts to discredit him and by the refusal of the Liberal government to lift measures of coercion. British influence was behind the Pope's instruction to disassociate from the National League and there had been a determined attempt to link Parnell with the Phoenix Park murders. This only served to consolidate the support of Irish people behind

Parnell. Now, rather than attack him, astute British politicians were making overtures to him. Both Joseph Chamberlain for the Liberals and Lord Randolph Churchill for the Conservatives were seeking political advantage from an accommodation with the Irish vote.

The Home Rule Crisis (1885–86)

The ultimate test of the constitutional approach would be the ability of Parnell to deliver some legislative independence for Ireland. This was enshrined in the concept of Home Rule. The beauty of it was its ambiguity. Because it could mean different things to different people, Parnell was able to sell it to the many different strands of Irish opinion. He was therefore deliberately vague about its implications. The minimum demand was for an Irish parliament for domestic affairs. As Britain would retain control over a number of important areas, such as defence and foreign policy, this could be presented to moderate opinion as a final settlement of the Irish question. It might even be accepted by Unionists as a way of saving the Union under a single British monarch. On the other hand, it could be presented as a means towards total separation. This interpretation allowed Parnell to keep more radical opinion in Ireland and America on board. He had to play a difficult juggling act which explains why he chose his words carefully depending on the audience he was addressing.

By 1885, the prospects for achieving Home Rule looked favourable. The franchise reform had trebled the Irish electorate to 600,000 by including agricultural labourers for the first time. The prospect of over 80 firm Parnellites was more a probability than a possibility. When Lord Randolph Churchill hinted that a Conservative government would see no need to renew coercion and would support the separate education of Catholics, the possibility of an accommodation with the Conservatives was opened up. The opportunity was taken in June 1885, when combined Irish and Conservative votes defeated the Liberals on a budget measure and forced the resignation of Gladstone's government. Lord Salisbury immediately took office as Prime Minister of a minority Conservative government.

While there was no formal agreement between the Irish and Conservatives, there were immediate benefits. Coercion was dropped and a land purchase scheme set up under Ashbourne's Act. The new Lord Lieutenant, the Earl of Carnavon, showed himself willing to negotiate some acceptable form of self-government for Ireland. Lord Salisbury, however, needed a secure majority and called the general election.

Parnell's tactics during the campaign were to listen to both sides to see how far each would go towards Home Rule. Joseph Chamberlain's Central Board scheme was given a fairly hostile reception as it seemed to offer local rather than national self-government. In any case, he failed to get the backing of his own Liberal leadership. Although the Conservative line on Home Rule remained suspect, Parnell decided to urge Irish voters in Britain to vote against Liberal candidates. He believed that the best chance of success still lay with the prospect of a strengthened Irish party holding the balance between the two major parties. His advice was aimed at avoiding the danger of one party having a majority without the need for Irish support.

Parnell's party gained every seat outside North-East Ulster including even a seat in Liverpool. Their total of 86 seats exactly matched the Liberal majority over the Conservatives (325–249). Events moved quickly. Although Parnell kept the Conservatives in power, Lord Salisbury made it clear that he was not prepared to concede Home Rule. After the election result, Gladstone's son had indicated his father's conversion to Home Rule. Having failed to get a working majority Salisbury indicated he was considering further coercion in Ireland. Parnell switched sides and put Gladstone in office. He immediately announced his intention to introduce Home Rule.

The consequences are well known. Even before Gladstone outlined his proposals to the House of Commons, Chamberlain had already resigned and the opposition of Lord Hartington, the leader of the Whig faction, was understood. The second reading of the bill was defeated in June 1886 by Liberal defections, 341 votes to 311. Gladstone dissolved parliament and an election was fought on the single issue of Home Rule for Ireland. The British electorate delivered its verdict – a solid rejection of Home Rule. The Conservatives and their Liberal Unionist allies won 394 seats to the Liberals' 191 and the Irish Party's 85.

The Liberal Alliance (1886–90)

Viewed with hindsight, the defeat of the Home Rule bill can be seen as the moment when the constitutional approach failed. The Conservatives had relaunched their political fortunes on the ticket of maintaining the Union. Their hold on power was secure and there was little prospect of the Liberals returning to office for the foreseeable future. Even if they did, any Home Rule bill would surely be defeated in the House of Lords by the inbuilt Unionist majority. Then there was the issue of the resolute opposition to Home Rule among the Ulster Protestants which threatened to be mobilised in 1886. It was only likely to harden.

It seems all the more remarkable then that Parnell's standing among Irish Nationalists at home and abroad was not only sustained but strengthened. Most considered the commitment of Gladstone and the bulk of his party as a positive gain and Home Rule would follow sooner or later. They chose to ignore the fact that the Irish Party had lost its independence and were totally reliant on the Liberals. Instead, the mood remained buoyant on the promise of Home Rule. Parnell could do little more than maintain the unity of Irish opinion.

During this period that unity survived attacks from a number of different quarters. Agricultural depression had once again set in and land agitation returned in the form of 'The Plan of Campaign', in effect a relaunch of the Land League. Parnell chose to distance himself from it while supporting the rights of tenants to keep their holdings. By doing so, there was the risk of alienating radical support especially in America. Instead, the Unionist government helped his cause by its aggressive use of coercion and its support of the campaign by *The Times* to link Parnell with the Phoenix Park murders (see Chapter 4). There was another attempt by the papacy to detach the Catholic Church in Ireland from the support of the national movement. Finally, constructive unionism (see Chapter 2), with its promise of radical land reform, threatened 'to kill Home Rule with kindness'. Instead, Parnell emerged stronger than ever. When it was revealed that the letters supporting the Phoenix Park murders he was accused of writing were forgeries, he was proclaimed as the 'uncrowned King of Ireland'. This time liberal opinion in England joined in the applause.

Parnell's fall (1890–91)

Just at the point when Parnell seemed to be at the height of his powers, Captain O'Shea sued his wife for divorce. The consequences were dramatic. A combination of forces destroyed the unity of the party, the liberal alliance and the prospects for Home Rule. Parnell's political career lay in tatters before his untimely death in October 1891. (See Chapter 5 for a full assessment of the factors which brought about his political fall.)

During the final few months Parnell continued to fight for his political survival. On a number of occasions he appeared to have abandoned his faith in the constitutional approach and appealed to the radical Fenian tradition. Certainly his increasingly violent speeches attracted Fenian support. However, this came just at the time when the mainstream support was deserting him. His candidates lost three by-elections in a row. His appeal to the 'hillside men' was the appeal of a desperate man. Even in his most desperate moods he couched his words in typical ambiguity. He knew there was no alternative to the constitutional approach. There were neither the resources nor the desire to raise a rebellion against British rule. Home Rule might be a faint hope but it was the only hope and it could only be delivered by an alliance with the Liberal Party.

So, during the twists and turns of his short political career, is it possible to reach any definite conclusions about what Parnell really stood for? It is clear that, despite his flirtations with the revolutionary strands of Irish nationalism, he used them for political ends. All his actions and speeches point to a commitment to constitutional rather than revolutionary means. But, as a means to what end? This is more difficult to answer. His belief in Home Rule is unquestioned, but whether he believed it was a final settlement is less clear. It seems reasonable to accept that he simply could not know and was genuine when he said that no man can fix the limit of the march of a nation, not even himself.

The following conversation is reputed to have taken place between Parnell and Davitt during the Home Rule crisis in 1886. If it is genuine, it is very revealing and consistent with the observations made by historians like Roy Foster and Paul Bew about the influences of Parnell's family and class background:

◢ Source

PARNELL ... I think that if we had a parliament in Ireland it would be wiser to drop the land question.

DAVITT Drop the land question! How could you drop the land question after all we have done during the last seven years?

PARNELL Oh! I don't mean that there should be no land legislation ... But there should be no revolutionary changes. No attack upon the land system as a whole.

DAVITT Mr Parnell! how on earth could you resist attacking the land system as a whole after your speeches? If you were Irish Secretary in an Irish Parliament, how could you defend yourself in the face of these speeches? What would you do?

PARNELL The first thing I should do is to lock you up.

Reported in R. Barry O'Brien, **The Life of Charles Stewart Parnell** *(London, 1910, 2nd edition)*

If we accept that a serious point was being made despite the obvious humour, Parnell provides us with a rare insight. He was musing about the nature of a future Ireland. Despite everything he had done to destroy his own class, he remained a landlord. Throughout his political career, he continued to take an interest in running his estate despite increasing financial difficulties. He considered himself to be an enlightened landlord who cared deeply about his tenants. It is not inconceivable to suggest that his vision of a future Ireland was one which looked for leadership from enlightened landlords like himself. It is somehow more convincing than the idea that Parnell would be happy to see Ireland at the mercy of an uncertain democracy.

TASK

You may be required by your exam syllabus to carry out some original research and produce a Personal Study. This is often the most enjoyable and rewarding part of the course, but can also be the most demanding and frustrating exercise. To produce a good personal study requires a number of different skills and great self-discipline. After all, although you will get help and guidance from your teachers, you are expected to use your initiative to decide the area of study, locate the sources you need, evaluate them and present your findings in a form which effectively communicates a sustained and supported argument. The whole process could take as long as 18 months. You will be given the final deadline for handing in your completed study, but you will have to manage your time and set your own deadlines to complete the various stages in the process.

There are two key points:
◢ The study must be manageable and must have a narrow focus.
◢ It must allow you the scope to get access to a wide range of both primary and secondary sources.

You may find that the topics covered in this book offer some possibilities. You could base a study around the role of individuals like Anna Parnell and Michael Davitt and the part they played in the Land War. You might consider one of Parnell's rivals such as Tim Healy and the part he played in Parnell's downfall. Alternatively, you could base a study around the influence of the Catholic Church of Ireland on a selected event. These are just a few suggestions. What they all have in common is manageability with a narrow focus and widely available sources.

Once you have considered a few options, your first call should be on the local library. Think of yourself as a detective. Once you have found one relevant book you have a number of leads. The bibliography will provide you with lists of other sources. The library is part of a national network. The British Library has a copy of every book published in Britain. It may take time but you can always order the books you need. Visit your local record office and museums. Staff are only too willing to help.

CHAPTER FOUR

'PARNELLISM AND CRIME'

Objectives

◢ To study the evidence presented against Parnell

◢ To establish the motives behind the campaign to discredit Parnell and the degree of involvement of the government.

On 7 March 1887, *The Times* launched its campaign to discredit Parnell. A series of articles followed, which tried to establish a link between Parnell's Party and terrorist violence and assassination. The constant stream of allegations put Parnell and his associates on the defensive and he was forced to deny them. The Conservative government used the opportunity to set up a Special Commission to investigate the entire record of the Irish Parliamentary Party and its links with land agitation, particularly during the Land War of 1879 to 1882. Witnesses were herded before the commission to establish the validity of *The Times'* case. If the intention was to discredit Parnell and his Party, it was a miserable failure. In fact, Parnell emerged from the affair stronger than ever with his reputation intact. The reason for this was that the focus of the attack upon him was in the form of letters alleged to have been written by Parnell implicating him in conspiracy to murder the Secretary and Under-Secretary for Ireland in Phoenix Park, Dublin in 1882 (see below). When it was clearly established that these had been forged by the ex-Fenian journalist Richard Pigott, the matter was settled in the public's mind. It hardly mattered that the commission's report effectively linked elements of the Land League with organised violence and intimidation.

It is the intention of this chapter to study the evidence closely, especially the articles themselves, to establish the motives behind the campaign and the degree of involvement of the government itself. As always, the sources must be placed in their precise historical context in order to tease out the reliable information they reveal.

◢ Source A

... There are volumes of evidence, and it is being added to every day, to show that the whole organisation of the Land League, and its successor the National League,

depends upon a system of intimidation carried out by the most brutal means and resting ultimately upon the sanction of murder ...

It may well be that at certain moments the murder of landlords and tenants is honestly discouraged by the League and the gentlemen who do its work in the House of Commons ... At the present moment, for example, it is not good policy to alarm the diminished party that still adheres to Mr Gladstone. They want very much to believe that Mr Parnell is the head of a constitutional agitation, that he is quite fit to be head of a nation, and that he has no desire whatever for separation ...

Mr Gladstone and his party are deliberately allying themselves with the paid agents of an organisation whose ultimate aim is to plunder and whose ultimate sanction is murder, to paralyse the House of Commons and to hand Ireland over to social and financial ruin ... Not long since, Sir William Harcourt [minister in Gladstone's Liberal government] *exposed the League's connection with 'Communism in Paris and Fenianism in America' and demonstrated its authentic doctrine to be 'the doctrine of treason and assassination'. Only 18 months back he was still convinced that 'the absolute separation of the two countries' was the aim of his present allies.*

The Times, *7 March 1887*

At the time the article in Source A appeared, the Plan of Campaign was in full swing. Its basic idea was to withhold excess rents and use the fund to protect evicted tenants. Although it was never on the scale of the Land War the similarities with it were clear for all to see. The return of recession in agriculture and the renewed threat of eviction were once again its immediate causes. When the Home Rule Bill was defeated the previous year, there was a realignment of British political parties. The Bill had been defeated by the defection of the Liberal Unionists. The general election appeared to confirm the opposition to Home Rule among the British electorate. Lord Salisbury took office as Conservative PM committed to maintaining the Union of Ireland and Great Britain. He needed to keep the alliance with the Liberal Unionists. He therefore announced his intention to govern Ireland firmly and deal with the return of land agitation by introducing a tough set of coercion measures. It was therefore in his interest to discredit the Home Rule alliance of Parnellites and Liberals. *The Times* could help justify coercion measures if publication of the most dramatic allegations coincided with the debates on coercion in the House Of Commons.

Later articles stressed the relationship between members of Parnell's party and radical Irish Nationalists in America. Particular emphasis was placed on the links between the treasurer of the Irish Party, Patrick Egan, and the outspoken editor of *Irish World*, Patrick Ford. The article of 10 March 1887 quoted Ford's attitude to the Phoenix Park murders. The ground was being prepared to implicate Parnell directly and time the publication of letters in its possession to gain maximum advantage for Lord Salisbury and his government (see Source B).

◢ Source B

He [Ford] *no longer thought 'the taking-off of Cavendish' a crime, or charged it against the landlords. 'From an Irish standpoint', he explained, it 'was an execution, not a murder.'* (Irish World, *23 June 1883).*

The Times, *10 March 1887*

Support for the newspaper's campaign came from letters sent to the paper. The following was significantly signed, WEST BRITON:

◢ Source C

… Within the last fortnight Ford has again made public profession of his faith in Mr Parnell. This man, who lives by advocating murder, tells us that he 'recognises Mr Parnell as the leader of the Irish movement both in and out of Parliament, and cheerfully gives him and the movement all the support in his power …

The Times, *18 March 1887*

The campaign was clearly aimed at unsettling the Liberals who could be portrayed as guilty by their association with Parnell and the cause of Home Rule. As supporters of the Conservatives and the preservation of the Union, it was equally important for *The Times* to prevent the reconciliation of Gladstone's Liberal Party and the Liberal Unionists led by Lord Hartington and Joseph Chamberlain. At the time of the extract in Source D, there had been a Round Table Conference held to discuss the possibility of reuniting the Liberal Party.

◢ Source D

... The avowed intimacy between Gladstonian Liberalism and the Parnellite faction must deepen the disgust at a base opportunism, the revolt against which has made the Liberal Unionists a power. Mr Chamberlain's speech at Birmingham proves conclusively there is no disposition to surrender their convictions in order to reunite the Party ...

The Times, *14 March 1887*

But the best was yet to come. On the morning of 18 April, the day set aside for the vote on the second reading of the Criminal Law Amendment Bill, the newspaper produced its trump card. To add to the dramatic impact it published a large copy of a letter supposed to have been written by Parnell to an unnamed person, dated 15 May 1882:

◢ Source E

Dear Sir,

I am not surprised at your friend's anger but he and you should know that to denounce the murders was the only course open to us. To do that promptly was plainly our best policy.

But you can tell him and all others concerned that though I regret the accident of Lord F. Cavendish's death I cannot refuse to admit that Burke got no more than his desserts.

You are at liberty to show him this, and others whom you can trust also, but not let my address be known. He can write to House of Commons.

Yours very truly,

Chas S. Parnell

Published in **The Times,** *18 April 1887*

Other letters followed including one which was to play such a crucial part in the course of events (Source F). The spelling mistakes are deliberately left in.

◢ Source F

Dear E,

What are these people waiting for? This inaction is inexcuseable. Our best men are in prison and nothing is being done. Let there be an end to this hesitency. Prompt action is called for. You undertook to make it hot for Forster and Co. [The Liberal Chief Secretary and his officials]. Let us have some evidence of your power to do so. My health is good, thanks.

Yours very truly,
Chas S. Parnell

A letter purportedly written to Patrick Egan, a member of an extremist group called the 'Invincibles' who carried out the assassinations of Lord Frederick Cavendish and Thomas Burke in Phoenix Park, Dublin. The letter was dated 9 January 1882, before the murders took place.

Parnell immediately denounced these letters as forgeries. However, denial was not enough; he had to find a way of clearing his name through some process of law. He wanted to sue *The Times* for libel, but was advised that cross-examination before an unsympathetic jury could be dangerous. The Liberal opposition pressed for an investigation by a select committee of the House of Commons. The Conservative government refused to consider it. It had its own agenda and was determined to extract maximum political advantage from the whole affair. It proposed and pushed through by Act of Parliament the setting up of a special Parliamentary Commission consisting of a number of judges. Instead of hearing the specific allegations against Parnell it was intended to widen the scope of the enquiry to investigate the whole history of the Land League in Ireland, Britain and America.

In all, 63 members of the Irish Parliamentary Party were named to answer charges against them. In addition, 67 other persons – extremists in Ireland and America – were named as associates of the accused MPs. Specific charges were made against Michael Davitt. He was accused of forming the Land League with money to be used for outrage and crime, and that he was the crucial link between the Parnellite party in Ireland and the revolutionary wing of the Irish-American nationalists.

The Special Commission began its proceedings in September 1888.

Counsel for *The Times* presented the outline of the case against the accused which the judges then summarised under nine headings. These were then used as the framework for the final report.

◢ Source G

These nine heads concerned three main issues. It was alleged first that the respondents were members of a conspiracy to bring about the absolute independence of Ireland. Secondly, that it was an immediate aim of the conspiracy to promote, by coercive methods and intimidation, an agrarian campaign against the payment of rents, with the object of bringing down the landlord system. And finally, that in pursuit of these objectives, the respondents either committed crimes themselves or were accomplices in crimes ... by assisting criminals and their dependants; by circulating, or allowing to be circulated, newspapers and other literature which incited to and approved of sedition, crimes, boycotting and other outrages; and by intimately associating with monstrous criminals and inviting and accepting help from advocates of crime and dynamite.

F. S. L. Lyons, **Charles Stewart Parnell** *(Collins, 1977)*

The government believed that by widening the scope of the inquiry it could weaken and perhaps destroy Parnell and the Irish Party and, in the process, damage Gladstone and the Liberals. It could justify its determined pursuit of law and order in Ireland against the Plan of Campaign and strengthen its own position as the party committed to the Union. There were many in the senior ranks of the party who were nervous about the tactics used. The Attorney-General himself, Sir Richard Webster, believed that by heading the case for the prosecution the government opened itself up to charges of collusion with *The Times* and political bias. Instead of winning greater public support it might have the opposite effect. Lord Salisbury, the Conservative PM, had no such reservations and insisted that Webster should vigorously pursue the case.

However convincing was the evidence connecting the Land League to violence and intimidation, the government had made a serious miscalculation. Public opinion was only interested in one issue – did Parnell write the letters attributed to him or not? On this crucial issue the case for the prosecution was at its weakest. Both the government and *The*

Times were too willing to believe that the letters were genuine. While it seemed to be common knowledge in Ireland that Richard Pigott, who supplied the letters to *The Times*, was unreliable and in desperate need of money, the paper was extraordinarily careless not to check the reliability of the source.

When Pigott was eventually brought before the Commission in February 1889 he was at the mercy of the defence counsel, Sir Charles Russell. In a dramatic and masterly example of cross-examination, Russell was able to reduce Pigott to a nervous wreck and expose him as a liar. Pigott was handed a piece of paper and asked to write down a number of words dictated by Russell. Almost as an afterthought, Russell asked Pigott to add the word hesitancy with a small 'h', as if that was the vital point. When the paper was returned to Russell it was revealed to the court that Pigott had spelt the last word, h-e-s-i-t-e-n-c-y.

Despite this dramatic revelation, Pigott had not admitted that he had forged the letters. It was expected that when the Commission reassembled on 26 February, Russell would deliver the final blow and extract the confession. But, Pigott was not in court; he had, in fact, crossed to France after signing two contradictory statements. One, amounting to a full confession, was read out in court (see Source H).

◢ Source H

The circumstances connected with the obtaining of the letters, as I gave in evidence, are not true. No one save myself was concerned in the transaction. I told Houston [an agent for *The Times* based in Dublin] *that I had discovered the letters in Paris, but I grieve to have to confess that I simply myself fabricated them, using genuine letters of Messrs Parnell and Egan in copying certain words and phrases and general character of the handwriting ... The second batch of letters was also written by me. Mr Parnell's signature was imitated from that published in* The Times *facsimile letter. I do not now remember where I got the Egan letter from which I copied the signature.*

Quoted in F. S. L. Lyons, **Charles Stewart Parnell** (Collins, 1977)

The prosecution immediately dropped the specific charges against Parnell who formally denied in front of the Commission that he had been the author of the letters. As for Pigott, he had made his way to

Spain from France to the Hotel Embajadores. The police were waiting for him. When they entered his room, he seemed to lose his nerve, placed a large revolver in his mouth and pulled the trigger.

It hardly mattered that the Commission's report, delivered in February 1890, concluded that *The Times* had successfully proved the links between the Land League and intimidation and the revolutionary elements of Irish-American nationalism. Parnell himself was cleared of all charges against him. Politically, the campaign against him had backfired. Parnell's standing in Ireland and Britain was never higher. The alliance with the Liberals was strengthened and public opinion was moving away from the Conservatives and towards Gladstone and the Liberals. In the libel case that followed, *The Times* was forced to pay £200,000 in damages and its reputation for accurate reporting was given a severe blow.

There remains a number of unanswered questions about the whole affair. Before his flight abroad, Pigott had written a second confession in which he claimed that he had not written all the letters. Although most observers were convinced that he was the sole culprit, Parnell was sure that the hand of Captain O'Shea was involved. He had worked closely with Joseph Chamberlain to supply evidence for the prosecution and even appeared as a witness before the Commission. The most intriguing fact of all was that he had arrived in Madrid the day before Pigott and was in the hotel when the unfortunate man committed suicide!

Moreover, it has been shown that the degree of collusion between the government and *The Times* was greater than was suspected at the time. *The Times* was provided with evidence for its case by government agents. Robert Anderson, head of the CID, not only supplied information, but even wrote some of the articles for 'Parnellism and Crime'. Most incriminating of all was the correspondence between *The Times* and the government even before the first assault was launched by the newspaper in March 1887 (see Source I).

◢ Source I

My dear First Lord,

A curious disclosure at a consultation with Sir Henry James yesterday evening compelled us at the last moment to postpone the announcement intended to be made this morning. It turns out that the letters had been under the highest legal consideration before being offered to us, and that the opinion pronounced upon them was that they were inadequate to sustain the case put forward.

I still feel firmly convinced that they are perfectly genuine documents and that much may be done to strengthen the weak points in them as evidence available in a Court of Justice. But more time is indispensable for this and meanwhile we must be silent.

Ever yours truly,

J. C. Macdonald

A letter dated 27 January 1887 addressed to W. H. Smith, the First Lord of the Treasury and Leader of the House of Commons from the manager of The Times. *Quoted in F. S. L. Lyons,* **Charles Stewart Parnell** *(Collins, 1977)*

This letter alone confirms that key government Ministers were kept informed of *The Times'* intentions and suggests that there was close cooperation between them. What is remarkable, given the note of caution in this letter, is that the paper proceeded to publish. This suggests that it was encouraged to do so by the government to advance its immediate political fortunes, although no explicit evidence exists to support this. However, such political considerations would explain why both the paper and the government were so ready to believe the letters to be genuine and why more time and care were not taken to check the reliability of their source. Political needs may well have clouded judgement.

TASKS

Answer the following questions on the sources in this chapter. Take care to read the sources carefully. Use the text to help you decide why each source was produced. This is especially important when you are asked to decide if a source provides reliable evidence for a given context. Always support your answers with precise reference to the sources.

1 What were the allegations made by *The Times* in Source A?

2 Do Sources A and B support the view that *The Times* was providing the Conservative government with political assistance? Explain your answer.

3 In relation to the content of Source C, why might the author of the letter have signed it, 'WEST BRITON'?

4 What was the specific aim of Source D?

5 Why might *The Times* have chosen 18 April 1887 to publish Source E?

6 Does the account of the cross-examination of Pigott by Russell prove that Pigott forged Source F? Explain your answer.

7 Source G was written by a modern historian. How far is it supported by Sources A, B and C?

8 To what extent is the reliability of Source H open to doubt?

9 Does Source I provide sufficient evidence of a conspiracy by *The Times* and the government to discredit Parnell?

10 What possible motives might *The Times* have had for launching its campaign against Parnell? Support your answer with evidence from the sources.

CHAPTER FIVE

THE FALL OF PARNELL

Objectives
◢ To understand the forces which contributed to Parnell's fall from power
◢ To assess the extent to which he contributed to his own downfall.

There is something very tragic about the story of Parnell's fall from power. It involved the rejection of him by a majority of his own party; the very party which he had done so much to create and build, and, worst of all, rejection by many of the Irish people themselves. It witnessed his desperate and futile battles to hold on to the leadership of both his party and Irish opinion. His early death soon after defeat in three successive by-elections was perhaps a fitting end to the tragedy. What's more, it followed so quickly on the heels of his greatest triumph: the collapse of *The Times'* case against him. There might perhaps be less sympathy for him if the trigger for the events which led to his fall was provided by the revelation of some sordid affair. Instead, his deep and passionate love for Katharine O'Shea was genuine. It is this picture of two people totally committed to each other in the face of a moralistic and hostile public which completes the tragedy.

The foundations of Parnell's power

We have seen that Parnell's achievement was to hold together under his leadership the various strands of nationalist opinion. This included almost unanimous popular support from the Irish people themselves, especially the tenant farmers, the most numerous group and even, perhaps grudgingly, acceptance of his leadership by the Catholic hierarchy. His dominance was built on his apparent mastery of the solid group of 86 Irish MPs of the parliamentary party. This unrivalled electoral success was ensured by a mature and skilled party machine organised in the constituencies by the National League, an organisation founded and led by him. Parnell even managed to retain the support of Irish American opinion despite its preference for a more extreme form of nationalism. Furthermore, he had succeeded in forging an alliance with one of the major British political parties and so provide a real prospect of Home Rule for Ireland. So difficult was the task that it has been described as being like 'riding a tiger'.

Shaking the foundations

When Captain O'Shea filed for divorce naming Parnell as co-respondent in December 1899, it was not realised that this would have the dire consequences for Parnell and Irish nationalism that it eventually did. After all, this was at the time when Parnell's position seemed unassailable after the collapse of the case brought against him by *The Times*. Not only was he more popular than ever in Ireland, but he had won many friends in England too. Public opinion was clearly moving in the direction of the Liberals as a string of by-elections had shown. Parnell had assured his friends that he would emerge from the divorce case as triumphantly as he had after Pigott's confession. Even after the embarrassing revelations of the divorce hearing itself in November 1890, the immediate reaction of nationalist opinion was to confirm its loyal support for Parnell and to silence his critics.

It is tempting to see the tragic consequences of the divorce case as inevitable. Once the nonconformist element in the Liberal Party denounced him and made it clear to the leadership that there could be no association with an adulterer, the Irish Party would have to choose between support for Parnell or the policy of achieving Home Rule through the alliance with the Liberal Party. They would, then, have no choice but to ditch Parnell because the alternative would be to commit political suicide. This is far too simple an interpretation of the unfolding of events. Such was the high regard for Parnell that there was every chance that he could withstand the unleashing of powerful forces against him. Certainly, he seems to have believed right up until the end that he could survive the crisis.

It was not, then, inevitable that the divorce case should result in his fall. It is not enough to point to the 'nonconformist' conscience as the sole cause of his demise. Given the nature of the Victorian moral code at the time, it was to be expected that public opinion in England should turn against Parnell. However, there remains the question of how that was handled by Gladstone and the leadership. No explanation would be complete without a consideration of Gladstone's actions during the months of crisis. Whatever the reaction in England, Parnell's power base was among Irish people at home and abroad. To understand his fall, we have to investigate the reactions of his fellow MPs in the party, the role of the Irish Catholic hierarchy, the Irish electorate and public opinion. Into the equation must be added the influence of Irish Americans. Finally, the decisions taken and the actions of Parnell himself require close scrutiny. Certainly, it is difficult to avoid the conclusion that things could have turned out very differently if Parnell had made different decisions.

Misjudging the mood

Parnell's confidence after the petition was filed seems to have been built on two factors. The first was that he had every reason to believe that O'Shea would be bought off and allow Katharine to divorce him. Parnell would then be free to marry the woman he had loved for ten years without a stain on his or her character. Secondly, he believed that his personal life was his own affair and had nothing to do with his public life. He was mistaken on both counts. O'Shea pursued the case without defence offered by the other side and the court naturally decided in his favour. In the process, the affair was laid open to public view portraying Parnell and Katharine practising all the deceptions usually associated with such affairs. Although there is good reason to believe that Captain O'Shea not only knew about the relationship early on, but even went along with it for his own reasons, this was not the verdict of the court and therefore not the version presented to the public. Even if it had been it seems unlikely that it would have made much difference. Parnell had miscalculated. What mattered was that he had been publicly revealed as an adulterer.

To the twentieth-century eye the Victorian moral code smacks of hypocrisy. There is no doubt that senior members of the Liberal Party, including Gladstone, had been aware of the affair for some time. The offence was not the affair itself but the public revelation of it. The reaction of the Nonconformists was almost immediate. The Rev. Hugh Price Jones made it clear that both the Liberal leadership and the Irish people should denounce Parnell. Gladstone was clearly deeply disturbed by this and was convinced that the Liberals would lose the next election if they did not distance themselves from the discredited Irish leader. How could they run an election campaign on a platform of Home Rule for Ireland with Parnell as Irish leader? How could they be seen to be offering control of a Home Rule parliament to someone perceived as immoral?

Gladstone conveyed these feelings privately to the vice-chairman of the Irish Party, Justin McCarthy, in the hope that Parnell would retire gracefully when it met to elect its leader and so avoid a public confrontation. There was a realistic prospect that Parnell could have retired from the scene until he was free to marry Katharine O'Shea, kept the alliance with the Liberals intact and resumed the leadership when the storm had died down. However, Parnell had no intention of standing down. He took the view that the independence of the Irish Party was all important and it should not be dictated to by any English leader. When the party met on 25 November, it was unaware of Gladstone's intervention. Parnell was re-elected unopposed. Despite their private misgivings, there were few Irishmen prepared to challenge Parnell's authority publicly at this stage. Even the Irish bishops, whose natural inclination was publicly to condemn an adulterer, kept silent. The National League confirmed its unswerving support for Parnell and a message from America endorsed the same view. It is ironic that the only public voice of dissent came from Michael Davitt. Even before Gladstone wrote his letter to McCarthy, Davitt had written an article in his *Labour World* warning of the threat to the Liberal alliance if Parnell continued as leader.

A cruel choice

It was Gladstone's decision to publish his concerns which forced the issue. Once the issue was out in the open, Irishmen could no longer pretend that there was no threat to Home Rule if Parnell was retained as leader. Already there were those in the party who voted for Parnell's re-election in the hope that he would retire with honour. They could now no longer stay silent.

◢ Source

... the continuance of Mr Parnell in the leadership of the Irish Party at the present moment would be, notwithstanding his splendid services to his country, so to act upon British sentiment as to produce the gravest mischief to the cause of Ireland; to place those who represent the party in a position of irremediable difficulty; and to make the further maintenance of my own leadership for the purposes of that cause little better than a nullity.

Gladstone's original letter to McCarthy, dated 23 November 1890, later published on 28 November. The meeting of the Irish parliamentary party which re-elected Parnell was on 25 November.

There is no question that Gladstone's decision to publish was an error of judgement. While he was under pressure to respond to the concerns of his own party, he had now pushed the Irish members into a corner. The chance of dealing with the crisis privately and persuading Parnell to stand down, at least temporarily, was now significantly reduced. Instead, the chances of an open rift in the party were increased. They were being given an impossible choice. Either they would stand by Parnell on the issue of Irish independence from any British interference or sacrifice Parnell in order to maintain the alliance with the Liberals and the cause of Home Rule. If they stayed loyal to Parnell, where could that lead? Since 1886, Parnell himself had made it clear that there was no alternative to an alliance with the Liberals to achieve Home Rule. It soon became clear that some in the party would go one way and some the other. Although the focus was naturally on the Irish members, every Irishman was being asked to make the same choice. It was likely that the emerging division of opinion in the party would also be reflected in the country as a whole.

What of Parnell himself? If Gladstone's action had been misguided, then Parnell's reaction was provocative in the extreme. He made it clear to a second meeting of the party that he had no intention of standing down. It was decided to adjourn this meeting to find out the views of others including Dillon and O'Brien who were in America collecting money for evicted tenants and reconvene on 1 December. Ahead of this meeting, Parnell took an extraordinary step. He decided to publish a 'Manifesto to the Irish People' (see following source).

◢ Source

The integrity and independence of a section of the Irish parliamentary party having been sapped and destroyed by the wirepullers of the English Liberal Party, it has become necessary for me, as the leader of the Irish nation, to take counsel with you, and, having given you the knowledge which is in my possession, to ask your judgement upon a matter which now solely devolves upon you to decide ... Sixteen years ago I conceived the idea of an Irish parliamentary party independent of all English parties ... I believe that party will obtain Home Rule only provided it remains independent of any English party. I do not believe that any action of the Irish people in supporting me will endanger the home rule cause, or postpone the establishment of an Irish Parliament ...

Published in **Freeman's Journal**, *29 November 1890*

Within the body of the manifesto Parnell gave details of a private meeting he had had with Gladstone suggesting that Gladstone was lukewarm on Home Rule. It is difficult to avoid the conclusion that Parnell had lost his political judgement. He must have realised that this would finish for good his own association with the Liberals and inflame those forces within Irish opinion which were already gathering against him. He must have believed that he could maintain control of Irish opinion by appealing to them directly over the heads of the party on the strength of his record of leadership. If he achieved the backing of the Irish people, he could use this to restore control of his party on the principle of independence from the Liberals. But there were serious flaws in this strategy. The political reality since 1886 was that independent action by the Irish Party could not exist. Home Rule could only be achieved in association with the Liberals. Until the divorce crisis no-one worked harder than Parnell himself to keep that alliance alive against threats from all sides. Could he really expect Irishmen now to ditch that policy and follow him into the wilderness? What alternative was he offering?

Perhaps an answer can be found in a speech he made in Ireland in May 1889 when he considered what might happen if Home Rule could not be won by constitutional means:

◢ Source

I for one would not continue to remain for twenty-four hours longer in the House of Commons at Westminster ... The most advanced section of Irishmen, as well as the least advanced, have always understood that the parliamentary policy was to be a trial and that we did not ourselves believe in the possibility of maintaining for all time an incorruptible Irish representation at Westminster.

*Quoted in Conor Cruise O'Brien, **Parnell and His Party** (OUP, 1957)*

The manifesto seemed to be returning to this theme by suggesting there was an alternative to the constitutional approach. Later, when the battle moved to Ireland, he seemed to imply that the alternative was a return to the Fenian tradition of direct action. However, this was a sterile alternative. Few, except the minority on the extreme wing, believed that much could be gained by force of arms against the might of Britain. It is most unlikely that Parnell believed so either. Instead, it is more the case that he felt his last chance was to use the emotional appeal of nationalist aspirations to lever the party in line behind his leadership. In that event, the Liberals would not be able to ignore a disciplined Irish party.

The wolves gather

If that was his strategy, he had miscalculated. The manifesto simply encouraged his opponents to declare their position. First to react was the American delegation led by Dillon and O'Brien who immediately cabled that the manifesto meant they could no longer support Parnell's leadership. More important still was the decision of the Catholic archbishops to break their silence. On the eve of the meeting of the party which would decide Parnell's future, Archbishop Walsh gave an interview to the Central News Agency (see next source).

◢ Source

... if the Irish leader would not, or could not, give a public assurance that his honour was still unsullied, the party that takes him or retains him as its leader can no longer count on the support of the bishops of Ireland. In speaking as I have spoken, I confine myself almost exclusively to the moral aspect of the case. If Mr Parnell can set himself right I raise no question as to the probable political results of yesterday's political

manifesto ... But ... I cannot but look upon the issuing of that document as an act of political suicide. It will bring disaster upon Ireland unless those whose duty it is to guard her interests are now faithful to their trust.

Interview with Archbishop Walsh in **Freeman's Journal**, *1 December 1890*

It is difficult not to agree with the Archbishop. The party would meet next day in the knowledge that the eyes of Irish people across the world were on them. They were not only representing themselves but the whole body of Irish opinion. The cable from America clearly undermined Parnell's position. Now, the intervention of the Church ensured that the moral issue could not be ignored after Parnell's attempt to distract attention from it. If Parnell fired the first shot in the battle for the hearts and minds of the Irish people, the Church had delivered a powerful counterblast. After the split arising from the party meeting which followed, the Church resumed its electoral role, but this time in support of anti-Parnellite candidates. Irish people were reminded that the Church remained the guardians of the strict Catholic moral code.

Despite Parnell's determination to carry the battle to Ireland, the deciding blow was delivered in Committee Room 15 of the House of Commons in the week following 1 December. The lead against him was taken by Tim Healey who argued that the cause of Home Rule was more important than any individual and that Parnell's leadership endangered it. Parnell was further criticised for his provocative manifesto. Parnell's supporters repeated the case against liberal interference and insisted on the principle of independent opposition. Most of the proceedings were conducted on a high level of political debate, but feelings ran high. Those who were not present never quite appreciated the highly charged atmosphere of the meeting and the emotions raised. The temptation to refer to the divorce was too great and this stirred Parnell and his supporters to anger. On the other side, there was frustration at Parnell's use of his position as Chairman to manipulate the proceedings. At the end of the week it was impossible to take a vote. Instead the party split in two when 45 members opposed to Parnell, including McCarthy as vice-chairman, left the room. Parnell was left with 27 supporters. It would take another 10 years before that rift was healed.

The futile battle

Parnell immediately took the battle to Ireland where by-elections were pending. Although he carried on the fight right up to his death in October 1891, the damage had been done. Parnellites and anti-Parnellites contested these elections which were marked by both verbal and actual violence. Parnell's candidates were decisively beaten at Kilkenny, Carlow and Sligo. On one occasion, Parnell had lime thrown in his eyes. The sheer physical strain of the campaign took its toll and friends commented on his physical and mental deterioration in the final months. He found it particularly hard to take the insults heaped on Katharine, whom he married in June 1891. He was provoked into replying to former colleagues in violent and abusive language. It had been war to the death and even his death left behind the bitterness of the split which could not be easily or quickly healed.

Conclusion

We have noted the complex interaction of forces which contributed to Parnell's fall, but it is difficult to escape the conclusion that he was largely responsible for it. After all, his involvement with Katharine was dangerous from the outset. It was bound to become public knowledge sooner or later and damage him politically in some way. He chose to ignore the fact that his personal life was a political issue as leader of a predominantly Catholic people who viewed marriage as sacred. What's more, he had cultivated an alliance with the English Liberal Party which saw itself as the conscience of the nation. He was unable to offer a realistic alternative to the Liberal alliance as the only vehicle to achieve Home Rule. His manifesto made it virtually impossible to avoid splitting both the Irish Party and public opinion. The only hope of maintaining the integrity of the party and keep the prospects of Home Rule alive was to sacrifice himself. He had the opportunity to do so at the outset and again when he was offered very favourable terms to resign during an attempt by Dillon and O'Brien to reconcile the two sides of the party. On both occasions, he obstinately refused to go. While it is rightly argued that his resignation would still have amounted to a fall, at least it would have been a defeat with his achievements intact in place of a scene of the Irish nation at war with itself.

This is not to excuse all others of some responsibility. Gladstone's decision to publish his condemnation of Parnell made it difficult for the party to find an agreed solution. He then refused to consider any compromise with the representatives of the Irish Party on Parnell's future role. The Liberal press revealed its insensitivity to Irish national feeling and opened Parnell's opponents to the charge of giving way to English force. There were those on the anti-Parnellite side who made any faint hope of reconciliation impossible by insulting Katharine O'Shea at every turn. Finally, the motives of the Catholic hierarchy were far from pure. There had always been a reluctance to accept a Protestant at the head of a predominantly Catholic nation and a resentment of the fact that the National League represented a rival and secular alternative to the traditional influence of the Catholic Church on public opinion in general and the Irish electorate in particular. There was no disguising the fact that many in the Church welcomed with relish the opportunity to re-establish its traditional political role. Despite all of these factors, Parnell's refusal to compromise stands as the most significant factor. Those qualities of resolute determination which had served him so well during the years of remarkable achievement were also largely responsible for his undoing.

TASK

Historians are not only concerned with **what** happened, but **why** events happened. For example:

▲ **Why** did the Great War break out in 1914?

▲ **Why** was there a revolution in France in 1789?

▲ **Why** did Parnell fall from power in 1891?

These are normally referred to as **causation** problems. Examiners are keen to ask such causation questions because they test the ability to provide clear **explanations** and **analysis** rather than straightforward **descriptions**.

A good analysis of causation has a number of key features:

1 The range of causal factors are clearly **identified**.

2 The **mechanism of cause and effect** is clearly explained. That means that the precise relationship between the identified factor and its consequences is made clear.

3 The answer shows clearly that these factors do not work independently of each other. Instead, they are interconnected in what historians often call a **complex web**.

4 Finally, the conclusion of the essay answer should attempt to consider the relative **importance** of the range of factors in bringing about the outcome. Here, it is not enough simply to state that one set of factors is more important than another. It is necessary to **establish** why some factors are more important than others.

Every essay answer needs to be planned. This provides a structure to work with to produce a clear **line of argument**. This means that decisions have to be made before you begin to write the answer. The following task should help you to find a clear structure for your answer and make those essential decisions.

Make a large copy of the diagram opposite. Use the material provided in this chapter to fill in the boxes with the factors which contributed to Parnell's fall. (A start has been made for you.) Then, think about the ways in which the individual factors are linked. You can draw lines between any two boxes which are linked. Finally, decide which factor or factors are the most important in bringing about Parnell's fall. To show the relative importance of the factors, draw arrows of different thicknesses from each box to the result in the centre.

TASK

This approach can, of course, be used for any causation problem.

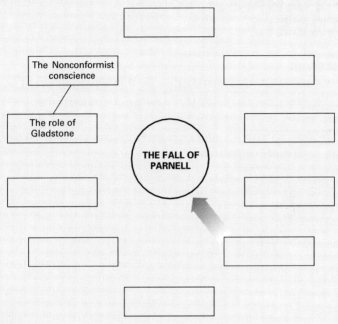

Figure 10

CHAPTER SIX

AN ASSESSMENT OF PARNELL'S CAREER

Objectives

◢ To understand the contribution made by Parnell to the development of the Irish Question in the nineteenth century

◢ To evaluate Parnell's successes and failures to form an overall assessment of his political career.

The Bishops and the Party
That tragic story made,
A husband that had sold his wife
And after that betrayed;
But stories that live longest
Are sung above the glass,
And Parnell loved his country,
And Parnell loved his lass.

W. B. Yeats, 'Come gather round me Parnellites',
*from **Last Poems, 1936–1939***

The short life of Parnell is so full of those ingredients which make for romantic fiction that the real Parnell is in danger of being lost in the myth which built up around him before his death and lingered on well after it. The circumstances of his fall during the last dramatic months have done much to feed the myth.

In his desperate attempt to gather support around him, Parnell appealed to the more extreme forms of Irish Nationalism. They, in their turn, repaid his memory by adding him to a list of Irish patriotic heroes cut down by Irish weakness and British treachery. He became associated with that strain of nationalism which stood for revolutionary and armed resistance against British tyranny and the desire for an independent Irish Republic.

The funeral was taken over by those who wished to paint him in their own image. So, the hurlers of the Gaelic Athletic Association – symbols of the new cultural nationalism of Irish separateness and Republicanism – provided the guard of honour. The inscription on his tomb – '*No man has the right to fix the boundary to the march of a nation ...*' – was deliberately chosen by those of the Fenian tradition.

It is the job of the historian to separate the myth from the reality. Indeed, there is general agreement among most modern commentators about the real Parnell. Conor Cruise O'Brien, F. S. L. Lyons, Robert Kee and, more recently, Roy Foster and Paul Bew have all made important contributions to a better understanding of the man. The figure which emerges is one very different from the myth. The real Parnell possessed enormous political skills and abilities, but also weaknesses. He left behind great achievements and yet he can be regarded as ultimately a failure. Either way, he had a significant impact on the future course of both Irish and British history and the relationship between the two countries.

His achievements were all in the field of practical politics. For that reason he should never be regarded as a revolutionary leader. Even his role as the leader of the Land League must be seen as part of a political strategy, to obtain the base of mass support he needed to gain control of the Irish Party at Westminster. The concept of the Land League as a popular movement to resist the power of the landlords and protect the interests of the tenants was Davitt's, not Parnell's. He simply used it and then abandoned it when it had served its purpose.

Even his most extreme speeches were carefully chosen to suit the audiences he was addressing and aimed to maintain his popular base, both in Ireland and America. His apparent appeals to the 'hillside men' during his last campaign were as carefully phrased as his earlier speeches and he continued to place his faith in the coming election.

It was therefore part of his achievement that he was able to present to Britain the image of a people united in a common aim behind his leadership. His creation of a disciplined, pledge-bound party organised in the constituencies by an elaborate party machine was perhaps his greatest achievement. Without this he would not have been able to make Home Rule a realistic prospect.

This was only possible because the two great British parties were forced to acknowledge the fact that there existed a third force which was capable of determining who was to hold power in Britain as a whole. From 1880 onwards, both Liberals and Conservatives had to look to Parnell's party as the expression of Irish opinion. The greatest prize and yet ultimately the source of weakness was the support of Gladstone and the Liberals for Home Rule.

There were prizes to be won from this strategy along the way. The Land Act of 1881 revolutionised the land problem and led the way to its eventual solution through the encouragement it gave to the idea of purchase by the tenants. While credit must be given to Davitt for the effectiveness of the agitation in Ireland, it was Parnell who was able to use it to bring political pressure on the British government. Before the creation of an independent Irish party, the interests of Irishmen could be largely ignored by the British establishment. Even the Unionists after 1886 continued to look for constructive solutions to the economic and social problems of Ireland.

This continued after Parnell's death but he takes some credit for the material progress experienced by many Irishmen from around the turn of the century. In particular, he would have approved of the work of the Department of Agriculture and Technical Instruction in supporting Irish industry.

However, for all his achievements he failed to deliver what the majority of Irishmen wanted. Home Rule may have been a very limited form of self-government but even that minimum expression of Irish independence did not become a reality. After 1886, the consequences of the Home Rule crisis meant that the Irish Party had lost its political independence.

Having staked everything on the constitutional approach, there was no alternative to the alliance with the Liberals. When that was shaken by the divorce, Parnell refused to accept that political reality. We have seen how he became the victim of his own strengths; how his iron will and determination to fight on became obstinate refusal to see the world as it really was.

Furthermore, he failed to define what was meant by Irishness and accept the fact that there were at least two Irelands. As a southern Protestant, he found it easier to relate to the concerns of Catholic tenants than to the sensibilities of Ulster Protestantism. Like so many Irish Nationalists he never came close to developing a constructive policy towards the northern Protestants, of how to deal with their determined opposition to the idea of Irish self-government.

There remained the anti-Catholic and anti-Irish feeling which was so deep-rooted in all classes of British, and, in particular, English society. Parnell never fully realised how deep that hatred was and how widespread was the view that the Irish were not fit to rule themselves.

He had much evidence of both in 1886 when the Orangemen reacted violently to the prospect of Home Rule and the British electorate gave its verdict in rejecting Gladstone on the single issue of Home Rule. Even when support seemed to be swinging back towards the Liberals, it did not mean support for Home Rule.

Finally, the return of a Liberal government did not guarantee self-government. As long as the House of Lords retained its veto, the inbuilt Unionist majority would ensure its defeat. In the unlikely event that the House of Lords could be pressured into accepting Home Rule, it was bound to be resisted by the Ulster Protestants as it was in 1912–14. If Parnell is to be judged in terms of his own stated goals, he was chasing an illusion.

The legacy he left behind was naturally coloured by the split and the bitterness of the conflict it caused. It is perhaps, therefore, too easy to lay emphasis on his failings. However, his achievements remain great simply because the context he worked in limited his freedom of action.

Until the divorce case he managed to hold together a complex assortment of forces against attacks from all sides and give Irishmen a sense of their own worth. Only O'Connell achieved anything comparable. Unlike O'Connell, Parnell refused to give in to British force. His impact on both Ireland and Britain was enduring.

His goal of domestic self-government as a solution to the Irish Question may never have been achieved, but he ensured that the desire for self-government, in whatever form it was expressed, was a political reality with which British governments would continue to have to deal.

Consider these questions on the Irish Question and the role of Parnell. They are typical of the kind of questions examiners like to ask. They all require much the same body of knowledge. The key is to use that knowledge to answer the question set:

1 **Why, and with what consequences** to 1850, was the Act of Union passed in 1800?
2 **To what extent** did the Famine change the nature of the Irish Question during the nineteenth century?
3 'The Kilmainham Treaty of 1882 marks the major turning-point of Parnell's political career.' **How accurate is this view?**
4 **How successful** was Parnell as Irish leader between 1880 and 1891?
5 **Assess** the impact of Parnell on British policy towards Ireland between 1875 and 1900.

It is important to be clear about what precisely each question is asking for. The key **direction** words have been highlighted:

1 **Why and with what consequences** ... There are of course two directions here.

The first is a **causation** question and asks you to explain the reasons behind the passing of the Act of Union. It should be treated in the same way as any causation question (see task at the end of Chapter 5).

The second part of the question directs you to consider the effects of the Act of Union. It requires identification of the effects on both Britain and Ireland.

A good plan would include a list of short-term and long-term consequences under the headings: social, economic and political. Just as the first part of the question requires a conclusion about the relative importance of the causes, so the second part requires you to weigh up the most important consequences. Each part of the question should be answered in turn to avoid confusion and each part should have a separate conclusion.

2 **To what extent** ... This very common phrase is asking you to measure. The alternative direction, **how far** ..., would mean the same thing. In this particular case it is asking you to measure the degree of change

either side of the Famine. A plan for such an answer should list those aspects of the relationship between Britain and Ireland which were changed by the Famine and those which were left unchanged. This should then provide a structure for an answer.

The conclusion should consist of a judgement about whether the degree of change is greater than the degree of continuity.

3 **How accurate is this view?** This type of question asks you to test an assertion or a point of view. It may be a quotation from an historian or one made up by the examiner. Whatever the case, the treatment should be the same. This particular view claims that Parnell's approach was fundamentally changed by his agreement with Gladstone. An appropriate plan would list the evidence for and against this view.

The plan should consider whether there were any other significant events which affected his approach. You must then decide whether or not you agree with this view or whether you would qualify it. Your decision then becomes the basis of your conclusion while the body of the answer debates the arguments on either side.

4 **How successful?** Faced with this type of question, it is vital to establish the criteria for judging the success and failure of a politician. As the direction asks you to decide if Parnell's achievements outweigh his failings, it makes sense to produce a plan which lists successes and failures on a balance sheet.

You can then weigh one side of the balance against the other to judge the degree of success or failure.

5 **Assess** ... This type of question also asks you to weigh up, or evaluate. Therefore the use of a balance sheet is once again appropriate. However, the headings for each side are not as obvious as for the previous question. As you are being asked to consider the role of an individual, it implies that the individual was responsible for certain aspects of British policy and that other individuals and other non-personal factors were responsible for others.

This time, you could use *Parnell* and *Not Parnell* as the headings for your balance sheet. As in the previous example, you can then weigh one side of the balance against the other. In this case, your judgement about whether it was mainly Parnell or other factors which determined British policy towards Ireland becomes the basis of your conclusion.

Using the suggestions above, construct a plan for each of the five questions. When you feel confident enough you should try to produce full written answers. Don't try to do too many in one go. One at each sitting should be enough.

FURTHER READING

The following bibliography can do no more than suggest some useful resources for those who wish to extend their knowledge and understanding of Parnell and the Irish Question, or to explore particular issues more fully.

The books are listed in alphabetical order of author. This is purely for convenience and does not reflect the value or interest of any of the various titles.

General histories

Paul Adelman *Great Britain and the Irish Question* (Hodder and Stoughton, 1996)

J. C. Beckett *The Making of Modern Ireland* (Faber and Faber, 1972)

D. G. Boyce (ed.) *The Revolution Perspective* (Routledge, 1991)

D. G. Boyce *Ireland 1828–1923* (Blackwell, 1992)

D. G. Boyce (ed.) *The Revolution in Ireland 1879–1923* (Macmillan, 1988)

George Boyce *Nationalism in Ireland* (Croom Helm, 1982)

Philip Bull *Land, Politics and Nationalism – A Study of the Irish Land Question* (Gill and Macmillan, 1984)

A. B. Cooke and John Vincent *The Governing Passion. Cabinet Government and Party Politics in Britain 1855–6* (Harvester Press, 1974)

R. F. Foster *Modern Ireland 1600–1972* (Allen Lane, 1988)

R. F. Foster *Paddy and Mr Punch* (Allen Lane, 1993)

J. L. Hammond *Gladstone and the Irish Nation* (Frank Cass, 1964)

Robert Kee *The Laurel and the Ivy, Parnell and Irish Nationalism* (Hamish Hamilton, 1994)

Robert Kee *Ireland, a History* (Weidenfeld and Nicholson, 1980)

Robert Kee *The Green Flag: A History of Irish Nationalism* (Weidenfeld and Nicolson, 1972)

J. Loughlin *Gladstone, Home Rule and the Ulster Question 1882–1913* (Gill and Macmillan, 1986)

F. S. L. Lyons *Ireland since the Famine* (Weidenfeld and Nicolson, 1973)

Oliver Macdonagh *States of Mind, Two Centuries of Anglo-Irish Conflict, 1780–1980* (Allen and Unwin, 1983)

T. W. Moody and F. X. Martin (eds) *The Course of Irish History* (The Mercier Press, 1984)

M. Winstanley *Ireland and the Land Question (1800–1922)* (Methuen, Lancaster pamphlet, 1984)

Biographies

Paul Bew *C. S. Parnell* (Gill and Macmillan, 1980)

D. G. Boyce and Alan O'Day (eds) *Parnell in Perspective* (Routledge, 1991)

E. Byrne *Parnell: A Memoir* (Lilliput Press, 1991)

Frank Callanan *T. M. Healy* (Cork University Press, 1996)

R. F. Foster *Charles Stewart Parnell: The Man and his Family* (Allen Lane, 1979)

F. S. L. Lyons *Charles Stewart Parnell* (Collins, 1977)

F. S. L. Lyons *The Fall of Parnell* (London, 1960)

Conor Cruise O'Brien *Parnell and His Party 1880–90* (Oxford University Press, 1957)

R. B. O'Brien *The Life of Charles Parnell 1846–91* (London, 1898)

Katharine O'Shea *Charles Stewart Parnell. His Love Story and Political Life* Vol. I (Cassell, 1914)

Articles

T. W. Moody 'Anna Parnell and the Land League', *Hermmathena* cxiii (1974)

Anna Parnell 'Tale of a Great Sham', Arlen House (1986)

INDEX

KEY TERMS

Fenians 13
Laissez-faire 43
Nonconformists 48
'Obstructionist' policy 15
Orangemen 17
Sectarian 52
Tithe 29

PROFILES

Butt, Isaac 24
Chamberlain, Joseph 26
Churchill, Lord Randolph 25–6
Davitt, Michael 25
Gladstone, William Ewart 24
Parnell, Anna 25
Stephens, James 24

MAIN INDEX

Act of Union (see also Union) 28–9, 32
Anglican Church (see also Church of Ireland) 28, 29–30, 32, 40, 48–9

Balfour, Arthur 20, 58, 59
Boycotting 16, 69, 70-4

Catholic Association 33, 37
Catholic Church 22, 28–9, 31, 39–40, 55, 66–8, 75, 78, 92, 98–9, 101
Catholic Emancipation 28, 32–5, 39
Church of Ireland 36, 47, 48–9
Coercion 17, 19, 33, 34, 36, 49, 53, 54, 57, 75–7, 78, 83–4
Constructive Unionism 57–60

Davitt, Michael 13, 16, 52, 69, 79–80, 86, 95, 105, 106
Dillon, John 20, 58, 74, 96, 98, 100

Famine 10, 28, 32, 39, 40–4
Fenians 11, 13, 14, 22, 44, 47, 61, 67, 79, 82–3, 98, 105

Gaelic Athletic Association 59, 105
Gaelic League 59
Gladstone, William Ewart 11, 17, 19, 22, 44, 46–62, 76–7, 83, 87, 89, 93–7, 101, 105–7
Grattan's Parliament 31

Healy, Tim 99
Home Rule 13, 14, 15, 18, 19, 20, 23, 47, 51, 55–7, 60–1, 65, 70, 76–7, 79, 83–4, 93, 95–6, 100, 105–8

Irish (Nationalist) Party 15, 16, 18, 19, 20, 22, 43, 47, 55, 58, 65, 67–8, 82, 84, 86–7, 92–101, 105–7
Irish National League 18, 55, 68, 74–5, 82, 92, 95, 101

Kilmainham Treaty 18, 54, 70

Land League 16, 18, 20, 21, 22, 53, 55, 58, 67, 69–70, 74, 82, 86–7, 89, 105
Land War 16, 17, 18, 47, 52, 53, 69–70, 82–3

Nationalist 15, 17, 22, 23, 32, 52, 55, 57, 58, 59, 61, 66–7, 84, 86, 98, 106
New Departure 15–6, 68–70

Obstruction 14, 68, 75
Orange Order 20, 36, 107
O'Brien, William 20, 58, 96, 98, 100
O'Connell, Daniel 33–9, 107
O'Shea, Captain William 3, 17, 21, 79, 89, 93–4
O'Shea, Katharine 3, 17, 18, 20, 21, 22, 23, 64, 92, 94–5, 100–1

Parnell, Anna 18, 69–70
Parnell, Charles Stewart (early life) 10–2; (political apprenticeship) 12–5; (and the New Departure) 15–8; (and Home Rule) 18–20; (and Nationalism) 64–80, 104; (fall of) 21–3, 92–101
Parnellism and Crime 20–1, 58, 82–90
Peel, Robert 33, 36, 38, 39–41
Phoenix Park Murders 17–8, 21, 58, 75, 78, 84–6
Pigott, Richard 82, 88–9
Plan of Campaign 20, 58, 78, 83, 87
Plunkett, Horace 59
Presbyterians 28, 29–30, 31, 36
Protestant Ascendancy 36–7, 39, 51

Repeal (of the Union) 35–9
Republicans 43–4, 67, 105

Salisbury, Lord 19, 56, 58, 76–7, 84, 87
Society of United Irishmen 31

The Times   20–1, 58, 78, 82–90, 92, 93
Tone, Wolfe   31

Ulster   16, 30, 50, 77–8
Ulster Unionists (see also Unionists)   61

Union   10, 28, 32, 35, 37, 38, 40, 48, 49, 51, 53, 57, 59, 78, 84, 87
Unionists   20, 51, 55, 56, 57–60, 66, 76–7, 78, 83–4, 106–7

Wellington, Duke of   34

Young Ireland   38, 43, 44

Longman History in Depth

Series editor: Christopher Culpin

Titles in the series

Hitler and Nazism (0 582 29736 2)

Causes of the Second World War (0 582 29650 1)

Stalin and the Soviet Union (0 582 29733 8)

Origins of the First World War (0 582 29522 X)

The Russian Revolution (0 582 29731 1)

Parnell and the Irish Question (0 582 29628 5)

Gladstone (0 582 29521 1)

Chartism (0 582 29735 4)

Oliver Cromwell (0 582 29734 6)

Charles I (0 582 29732 X)

Henry VII (0 582 29691 9)

Addison Wesley Longman Limited,
Edinburgh Gate, Harlow,
Essex,CM20 2JE, England
and Associated Companies throughout the world.

The right of Tim Hodge to be identified as the author of this Work has been asserted by him in accordance with the Copyright, Designs and Patents Act of 1988.

First published 1998
© Addison Wesley Longman Limited 1998

Set in 9.5/13pt Stone Serif
Produced by Addison Wesley Longman Singapore Pte Ltd
Printed in Singapore

ISBN 0 582 29628 5

Acknowledgements

We are grateful to the following for permission to reproduce photographs:

The Fotomas Index, page 26; *The Graphic* 14. 1. 1882, pages 71, 72, 73, 74; The Hulton Getty Collection, pages 4, 11, 24, 25.

Cover painting: The Lobby of the House of Commons by Prosperi. Sotheby's Picture Library.

The publisher's policy is to use paper manufactured from sustainable forests.